TOP 10 CORNWALL AND DEVON

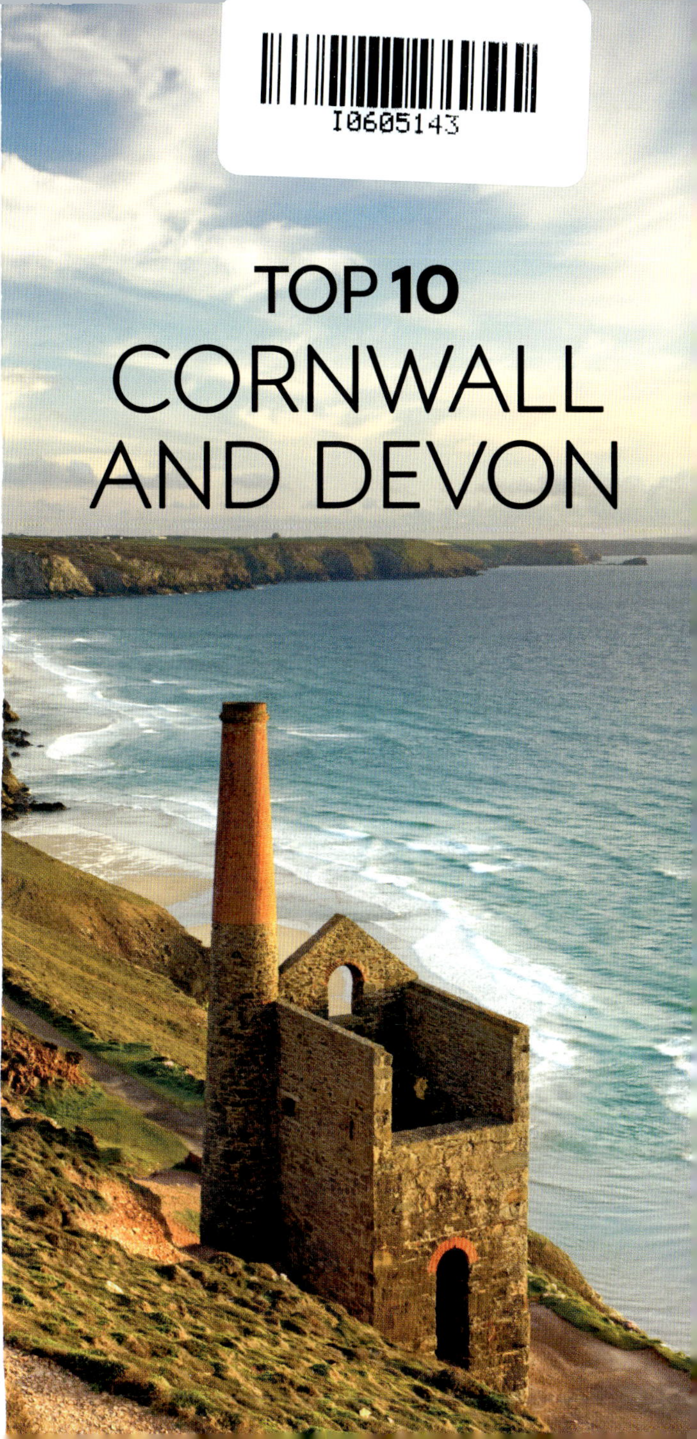

CONTENTS

44

Top 10 of Everything

72

Area by Area

108

Streetsmart

CORNWALL AND DEVON

INTRODUCING

Boats moored at Mevagissey

WELCOME TO **CORNWALL AND DEVON**

Spread across Britain's southwestern tip, the counties of Cornwall and Devon are famed for their coastal scenery, but there's even more to see beyond the seaside. Don't want to miss a thing? With Top 10 Cornwall and Devon, you'll enjoy the very best this region has to offer.

Even a short foray into Cornwall and Devon makes it clear why these far-flung counties have inspired generations of writers and artists. As local Agatha Christie wrote of Devon in *And Then There Were None*, "it really is lovely here … everything so green and luscious looking", and that's true of both counties. Devon's rolling countryside is a pastoral idyll, with

Cornwall's Cadgwith Cove

quiet valleys, sweeping sandy beaches, farmers' fields and the rugged wilds of Dartmoor painting a distinctly rural picture. Cornwall (the land of Arthurian legends) has a touch of something wilder, but no less beautiful. Here, windy bays draw crowds of surfers, rugged cliffs provide super-scenic walking and tropical botanic gardens, like the Eden Project, feel almost otherwordly.

Though the siren call of the outdoors is strong in both regions, there's plenty to do closer to civilization. Cornwall and Devon's cities are beloved for their top-notch restaurants and independent shops, plus a host of historic sites: there's Exeter's Gothic cathedral and Roman walls, Plymouth's naval history and Truro's excellent county museum. The coast and countryside are dotted with charming towns and villages, too, from genteel Sidmouth to quirky Totnes, and buzzy Falmouth to picturesque Padstow. And, perhaps favourite of all, St Ives, a bustling maze of art galleries and stylish bars.

So, where to start? With Top 10 Cornwall and Devon, of course. This pocket-sized guide gets to the heart of the region with simple lists of 10, expert local knowledge, and comprehensive maps, helping you turn an ordinary trip into an extraordinary one.

THE STORY OF **CORNWALL AND DEVON**

Various invaders may have had a hand in shaping Cornwall and Devon, but regardless of who ruled them, both counties have fiercely held onto their independence and unique local culture. Here's the story of how they came to be.

Ancient Roots

Cornwall and Devon have been inhabited for tens of thousands of years, as testified by the embarrassment of prehistoric ruins found across their ancient landscapes. There's evidence of people living here as far back as the Paleolithic period (a 40,000-year-old jawbone was found at Kents Cavern), followed by hunter-gatherer communities, who started to appear in the Mesolithic era. By the Neolithic era, numerous settlements had taken shape.

Agriculture didn't take hold until the Bronze Age (c 2400–800 BCE), alongside the region's first forays into mining (namely tin). During this time, locals were living in roundhouse settlements, but by the Iron Age (thanks to technological advances), hillforts were a common sight around the region.

Roman Britain

After the Roman Conquest of 43 CE, Romanization began to spread through Great Britain. Though it began in the south, Devon and especially Cornwall were far enough from the main loci of power that the Roman influence wasn't strong in the region. The area to the west of the River Exe – covering much of Devon and all of Cornwall – remained largely independent, inhabited by the Brittonic (Celtic) Dumnonii people. Their society remained much as it was before the Romans' arrival, with stone

A burial mound dating from the Neolithic era

Exeter Castle, built into the city's Roman walls

houses like those at Carn Euny still inhabited well into the Roman era. Yet one area witnessed significant Roman development: Isca Dumnoniorum (now Exeter, in East Devon) became a key fortified town during this time.

The Fall of Dumnonia

After the Romans' withdrew from Britain around 410 CE, Devon and Cornwall – now known as the Kingdom of Dumnonia – again stayed fairly independent. The Saxons and other Germanic peoples attempted to settle the area, but the Dumnonii retained their way of life and continued trading with other Celtic peoples. Over this period, their shared Common Brittonic tongue began to diverge and the Cornish language developed.

It was the Kingdom of Wessex that eventually conquered the area. Geraint, the last king of a unified Dumnonia, was defeated by the Wessex king Ine in 710, and the last-known Cornish king, Donyarth, died in 875. Not long after (in 1066), William the Conqueror secured the region under Norman rule. Though there was plenty of unrest in the following Middle Ages – including an 1138–53 civil war in England and Normandy and the arrival of the Black Death in 1348 – there was also a cultural renaissance. The Arthurian chivalric romance Tristan and Iseult appeared around the 12th century, and by the 14th century, a distinct Cornish literature had emerged.

Moments in History

38,000 BCE
Modern humans begin to inhabit the region, as shown by a fragment of jawbone (the oldest fossil of a modern human found in northwest Europe) unearthed in Kents Cavern in 1927.

55 CE
Isca Dumnoniorum (modern-day Exeter) is established by the Romans as their base of power for the region.

875
Donyarth, the last-known Cornish king, dies. Cornwall is subsumed into the Kingdom of Wessex around this time.

1068
Following the Norman Conquest, William the Conqueror lays siege to Exeter. The city withstands the attack for 18 days, finally negotiating an honourable surrender.

12th century
The tale of Tristan and Iseult, a Cornish knight and Irish princess, emerges.

1755
A tsunami caused by the Lisbon Earthquake hits the Cornish coast.

1830s
Cornwall's long-standing smuggling economy begins to decline, with changes to excise fees on imported goods and a more active coastguard service.

1951
Dartmoor becomes one of the first three National Parks designated in the UK, followed by Exmoor three years later.

1998
Cornwall's last tin mine, South Crofty, closes. Over the following years, periodical proposals to reopen one or more mines arise.

2002
Following a revival in the 20th century, Cornish is listed as a UK regional language by the European Charter for Regional or Minority Languages.

Uprisings and Unrest

The Tudor period was marked by civil unrest in Cornwall and Devon. Rising tensions due to economic hardships and the outlawing of tin mining led to the 1497 Cornish Rebellion, in which miners marched on London – gathering support in Devon as they went – only to be defeated at the Battle of Deptford Bridge. Later that year, the Second Cornish Rebellion formed around Perkin Warbeck, a pretender to the throne of King Henry VII. This too was defeated.

Tensions flared again in 1549 in the Prayer Book Rebellion. The Act of Uniformity decreed that everyone must use the new Protestant Book of Common Prayer, and hold services in English. This, combined with resentment and desperation after years of economic hardship, sparked a rebellion in the West Devon village of Sampford Courtenay, which was only suppressed after two months and over 5,500 deaths.

A century later, the English Civil War broke out, and while Devon's cities were largely on the victorious Parliamentarian side, the county's rural areas and most of Cornwall supported the Royalist cause.

All this conflict – combined with the 17th-century Little Ice Age and a smallpox epidemic – devastated the local populace, and was a key factor in the decline of the Cornish language.

Legal and Illegal Trade

Life in the region started to improve in the 18th and 19th centuries. Agriculture became Devon's largest industry and Plymouth grew into the county's largest city, as well as a vital naval port. Mining remained important in both counties, reaching its peak in the early 19th century. The Miners Association was formed in 1858, and the Camborne School of Mines in 1888. But by this time, tin reserves were low, and graduates left for mines overseas. Mine after mine closed, and locals had to find other means of making money.

Smuggling became a major source of income in the 18th and 19th centuries. Some 10,000 people are thought to have been involved in Cornish smuggling in its heyday, bringing in goods at remote coves and trafficking them through spots like Bodmin Moor's Jamaica Inn pub, all in order to avoid the high import duties on goods from mainland Europe.

Locals protesting second-home ownership in St Ives

Cornwall and Devon Today

The 20th century saw the arrival of a more reputable source of income in Cornwall and Devon: tourism. Rising in place of traditional industries in the region (fishing dramatically declined and mining was on its last legs by now), tourism became a lifeline for many. Dartmoor and Exmoor were classed as National Parks in the 1950s, and scenic spots like Torbay – marketed as the "English Riviera" – attracted domestic holidaymakers in droves. Artists had already been drawn to the area, with the Newlyn School emerging in the late 19th century, and the region soon became known as a haven for creatives. And while World War II brought heavy bombing to cities like Exeter and Plymouth, much of the region was spared this destruction.

Yet Britain's southwestern counties remain among its poorest, and while tourism has become economically essential, it's not without its complications. Second-home ownership has driven up prices for locals and many have been forced to move outside the region. However, things are looking up: with increased taxes on second-homes – and many second home-owners now debating selling up – locals may be able to once again settle in the counties they call home.

Depiction of the Prayer Book Rebellion in 1549

TOP 10 EXPERIENCES

Planning the perfect trip to Cornwall and Devon? Whether you're visiting for the first time or making a return trip, there are some things you simply shouldn't miss out on. To make the most of your time – and to enjoy the very best this scenic region has to offer – be sure to add these experiences to your list.

1 Walk the South West Coast Path

This lengthy trail *(p59)* follows the epic coastline of Cornwall and Devon, plus some of Dorset and Somerset. It's well established and well signposted, making it an easy and rewarding route to follow, whether you have a whole week or just an afternoon to spend walking.

2 Savour super-fresh seafood

Cornish crab, hefty oysters, fresh haddock: Cornwall and Devon are full of must-try fish and seafood. Want to sample it straight from the sea? Head straight to the harbour in towns such as Newquay *(p76)* to find small restaurants selling their morning catch.

3 Wander grand estates

Both counties have a rich selection of country houses and gardens. Standout stately homes include medieval Cotehele *(p82)* and High Victorian Lanhydrock *(p22)*, while beloved gardens include the neat lawns of Mount Edgcumbe *(p84)* and the magical Lost Gardens of Heligan *(p82)*.

4 Step back in time

Cornwall and Devon were long independent from the rest of England, and the remnants of their Celtic cultures are dotted across the land. Head to ancient sites such as the Merry Maidens standing stones *(p91)* and Chun Quoit (a neolithic chamber tomb; p91) for a glimpse into the past.

5 Marvel at the Eden Project

This incredible project *(p24)* was created by transforming a disused clay pit into a startlingly lush garden, with biomes maintaining different climates. The site also hosts summer concerts and features outdoor artworks.

6 Enjoy Cornish art

Loved for its light, West Cornwall has long been a haven for artists, and it still is today. Tick off top sights in St Ives *(p30)* – where you can visit Tate St Ives, the Barbara Hepworth Gallery and Leach Pottery – or explore the award-winning Falmouth Art Gallery *(p49)*.

7 Spot local wildlife

The Cornish coast promises a host of wildlife, such as whales, dolphins and seals, as well as birds like puffins. Inland, keep your eyes peeled for Dartmoor's "Little Five": the blue ground beetle, cuckoo, marsh fritillary butterfly, otter and ash black slug.

8 Hit the beach

Cornwall and Devon are famed for their beaches, and rightly so. Sandy stretches – like Fistral Bay *(p56)* – cover the coast, drawing sunseekers aplenty, but there are quieter spots, too. Head to coves on the Roseland peninsula *(p59)* to escape the crowds.

9 Try a cream tea

When it comes to this West Country staple, there's one big question: should you spread the indulgent clotted cream onto the scone first, or the sweet, tangy jam? Try both the Cornish (jam first) and the Devonian (cream first) ways, then decide for yourself.

10 Take to the waves

Surfing, bodyboarding, SUP, windsurfing, kayaking: there are so many ways to enjoy the sea in Cornwall and Devon. Head to watersport hubs such as Watergate Bay *(p56)* and Exmouth *(p105)* to learn the necessary skills before hitting the waves.

ITINERARIES

Surfing off the Atlantic coast, admiring historic buildings, dining on just-caught seafood: there's a lot to see and do in Cornwall and Devon. These itineraries offer ways to spend 4 days exploring Devon on public transport, or a week driving in Cornwall.

4 DAYS IN DEVON

Day 1

There's hardly a more epic place to start your Devon adventure than on the Jurassic Coast. Exmouth *(p105)* makes for an ideal base, with its red cliffs and sandy beaches perfect for a morning walk. Next, hire a bike in town and cycle along the riverside Exe Estuary Trail to Lympstone. You can refuel with a pub lunch here – or splash out at the Michelin-starred Lympstone Manor's Pool House restaurant *(p107)*. After lunch, continue cycling upriver to Exeter *(p38)* and drop off your bike (one-way cycle hire is possible on the trail). Spend the evening exploring the city, and have dinner at The Prospect Inn *(p64)*; it has sunset views and delicious food.

Cyclists on the scenic Exe Estuary Trail

EAT
The floating River Exe Café (open April–Sep) is one of Devon's more unusual places to eat. Your booking includes not only a table, but a spot on the water taxi from Exmouth – unless you'd rather canoe or paddleboard over.

Day 2

Take the 173 Stagecoach bus from Exeter to Dartmoor *(p36)* – of the four daily departures, you'll want to be on one of the two earliest. Stop first at Castle Drogo *(p46)*, an unusual 20th-century homage to medieval castles, then hop on the 173 again to the stannary town of Chagford. Treat yourself to afternoon tea at Michelin-starred Gidleigh Park *(p107)*, then head out for a hike on the moor. The circular Meldon Hill Walk, accessible from Chagford, will lead you up its eponymous hill, offering stunning views of this wild landscape. Catch the last bus back to Exeter for dinner – Harry's Restaurant is a local go-to *(harrysrestaurants.co.uk)*.

Day 3

In the morning, hop on the train to Totnes *(p105)* and soak up the atmosphere in this quirky town. Exploring its shops and galleries is the best way to discover its charms, but don't miss th view from the ruined castle or the beautiful St Mary's Church, either. After lunch at one of the excellent vegetarian restaurants here – Seeds 2 Totnes *(seeds2totnes.co.uk)* is a great option – take a river cruise down the lovely Dart Valley (cruises run from April to October; take the 92 Stagecoach bus if not in season). You'll reach the pretty town of Dartmouth *(p105)* in less than two hours (that's ample time to explore before a local pub dinner).

Day 4

On your final day in Devon, make the short hop across the river to Kingswear, from where you can ride the nostalgic Dartmouth Steam Railway *(p61)*. Stop at Greenway Halt if you're a big Agatha Christie fan – Greenway *(p106)*, her holiday home, is located here – if not, ride to the final stop, Paignton. You could squeeze in a detour to Brixham *(p105)*, the most charming of the Torbay towns, or spend your last night lingering in breezy Paignton. For seafood, you can't go wrong with the Harbour Light *(harbourlightpaignton.co.uk)*.

Boats moored at the harbour in Brixham

TRANSPORT

Buses are a great alternative to travelling by train around Devon, but they're not always predictable. Always plan ahead, check services on the day and allow some extra time.

7 DAYS IN CORNWALL

Day 1

With its sandy beaches, scenic river and quaint canal, Bude offers a great introduction to Cornwall and the county's love of the great outdoors. It's a place to enjoy the water: hit the waves on a surfboard, stroll along the towpath or hire a canoe to glide along the gentle canal. Be sure to take the cliff path up to Compass Point, too – the swoonworthy coastal views here offer a taste of what's to come.

Day 2

Start your day by driving along the Atlantic Coast to mystical-feeling Boscastle *(p76)*. An air of magic seems to linger around this little village, most keenly felt in the dramatic ruins of Tintagel Castle *(p74)* – forever linked to tales of the legendary King Arthur – and the intriguing Witchcraft Museum *(p49)*; the surrounding waterfalls, wooded river valleys and craggy coves are equally enchanting. Spend the day exploring the sights and walking through this wonderful landscape. Then, it's time for dinner at Tintagel's Ye Olde Maltehouse *(malthousetintagel.com)* for more Arthurian vibes.

Day 3

The next morning, drive to St Austell to see one of two spectacular gardens nearby: the Eden Project *(p24)* and the Lost Gardens of Heligan *(p82)* – both have good lunch options, too. Afterwards, take a stroll along the Clay Trails route that meanders past both gardens before driving down to ever-busy St Ives *(p30)* in Cornwall's far west. End the day with a seafood dinner at the smart Porthminster Beach Café *(p93)*.

SHOP
The Leach Pottery in St Ives *(p31)* is a museum housed in the home and workshop of revered potter Bernard Leach. It also has an excellent shop.

Day 4

Spend the morning enjoying St Ives' beaches (Porthmeor, Porthminster and Porthgwidden). Restless sunbathers could take a surf lesson instead, or hop on a boat trip to see the seals on the island of Godrevy. Find a cosy spot for lunch back in town – there are some great options in the lanes, like Blas Burgerworks *(p93)* – then immerse yourself in art at Tate St Ives *(p49)* and the Barbara Hepworth Museum and Sculpture Garden *(p49)*. For an atmospheric end to the day, hunker down in the 700-year-old Sloop Inn *(p92)*.

Day 5

Continue your journey southwest by driving to Penzance *(p32)*. The town is beloved for its unusual buildings (don't miss the Egyptian House and Market House), alongside other highlights like the open-air Art Deco Jubilee Pool. After exploring, grab a healthy lunch at Archie Brown's *(archiebrownscornwall.co.uk)* before heading out of town to see the iconic St Michael's Mount *(p32)*. Return to Penzance for dinner and try the tasting menu at The Shore *(theshorerestaurant.uk)*.

Day 6

Rise early to drive to Lamorna Cove Café *(lamornacove.com)* for breakfast. Then, it's time to travel back in time. Some of the best prehistoric sites in Cornwall are a short drive from here, including the Tregiffian burial chamber *(p91)* and the Merry Maidens stone circle *(p91)*. After gazing at these ancient ruins, pitstop for lunch in the port of Newlyn *(p90)*, then make your way back to Penzance.

Day 7

End your Cornish adventure in one of the region's most popular spots, Falmouth *(p26)*. Packed with great galleries and buzzy bars, this artsy town is a lovely place to wander around; it's also famed for Falmouth Art Gallery *(p49)* and Pendennis Castle – be sure to see both. For a farewell dinner, take your pick of the town's restaurants (there are too many good ones to name).

Falmouth's stunning Pendennis Castle

TOP 10 HIGHLIGHTS

St Michael's Mount, near Penzance

EXPLORE THE HIGHLIGHTS

There are some sights in Cornwall and Devon you simply shouldn't miss, and it's these attractions that make the Top 10. Discover what makes each one a must-see on the following pages.

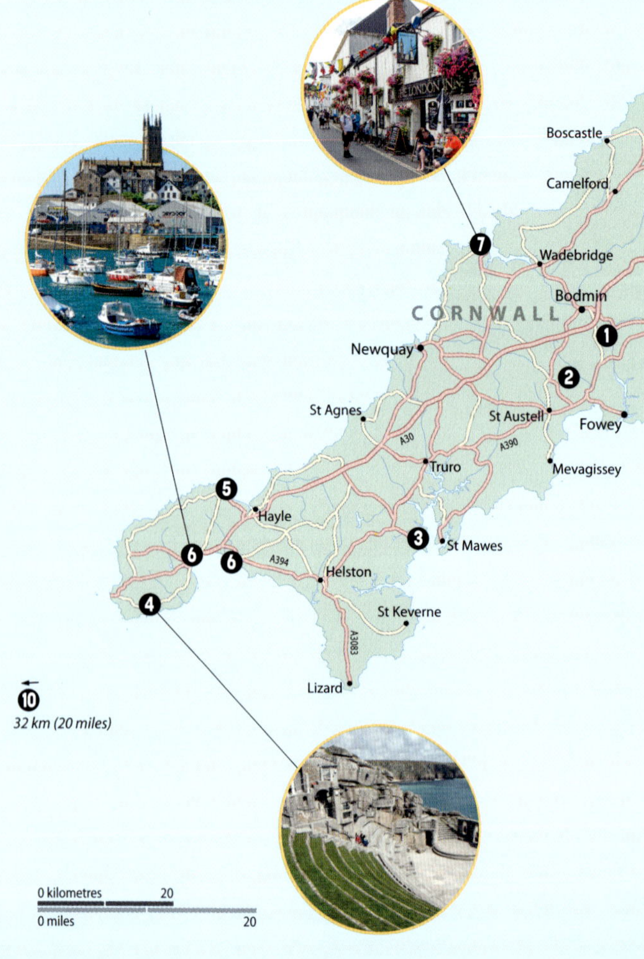

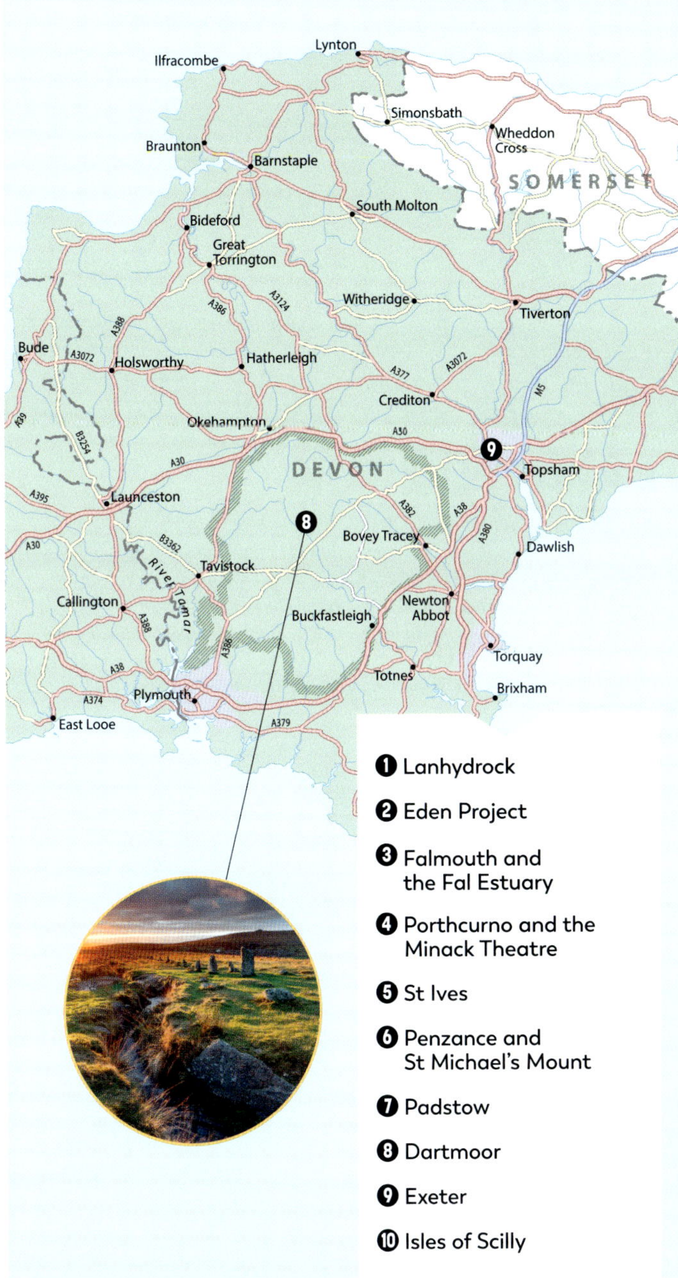

❶ Lanhydrock

❷ Eden Project

❸ Falmouth and the Fal Estuary

❹ Porthcurno and the Minack Theatre

❺ St Ives

❻ Penzance and St Michael's Mount

❼ Padstow

❽ Dartmoor

❾ Exeter

❿ Isles of Scilly

1

LANHYDROCK

D4 · Near Bodmin, Cornwall · Mar & Oct: 11am–5pm daily; Apr–Sep: 11am–5:30pm daily · nationaltrust.org.uk

This magnificent 17th-century mansion in the Fowey Valley is one of England's grandest country houses. Built by a rich merchant, Sir Richard Robartes, and reconstructed in 1881 following a disastrous fire, it remained in the same family until the National Trust took it over in 1953. Its 50 rooms offer a glimpse into life in a stately home.

1 Long Gallery

Lanhydrock's pièce de résistance, occupying the entire first floor of the north wing, is its epic plaster ceiling, which illustrates many stories from the Old Testament.

Jacobean plaster ceiling, Long Gallery

2 Nursery Wing

A whole suite of rooms, called the nursery wing, was set aside for bringing up the younger family members. The nursery itself is filled with play-things, including a large doll's house and a rocking horse, among many other toys.

3 Billiard Room

This spacious room exudes the spirit of the leisured life of the gentry with its billiard table and tiger-skin rug set against oak panelling. Old school photos and other such mementos line the walls.

EAT

The estate offers a variety of dining options, including the Courtyard Restaurant, a café near the car park, and a tea-room in the stables.

4 Captain Tommy's Bedroom

A suitcase kept on the cast-iron bed contains the personal items of Thomas Agar-Robartes, who died at the Battle of Loos (France) in 1915.

5 Kitchen

At the heart of the building is the main

Immaculate garden at the estate

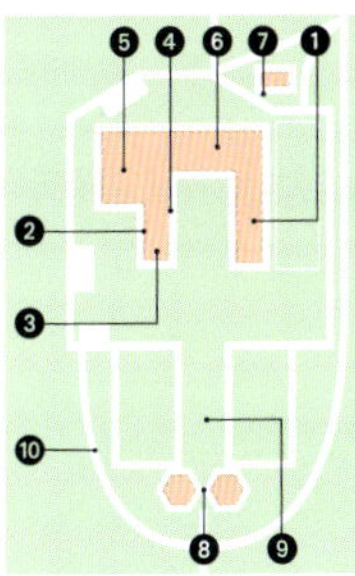

Lanhydrock Site Plan

kitchen, where the cook and servants worked. Its vast interior resembles a church, with soaring rafters and a gabled roof.

6 Dining Room

Decorated with stunning blue-and-gilt wallpaper designed by English textile artist William Morris, the dining room offers a glimpse into the life of the upper class in the Victorian era. A grand table, set for a formal meal, takes centre stage in the room.

7 St Hydroc Church

Dedicated to an Irish missionary, the church adjoining the house dates from the 15th century. A plaster panel in the north aisle displays the arms of King James I and is dated 1621.

8 Gatehouse

This pinnacled structure was built around 1650. The main room on the upper storey was used to entertain ladies while the men hunted. It leads into the Topiary Courtyard.

9 Gardens

There's much to see in the gardens *(p55)* at Lanhydrock, from vibrant herbaceous borders and a sparkling stream to a croquet lawn. The clipped yew trees and geometric flowerbeds are undoubtedly striking, but it is the magnolias in the shrub garden for which the estate's gardens are most renowned.

BELOW STAIRS

More than any other house of its period, Lanhydrock provides an intriguing insight into how a grand mansion operated. Passages lead from the main kitchen, with its elaborate ranges and gleaming copper, to sculleries, larders, a bakehouse and a dairy. At the top of the house are the nurseries and the servants' modest quarters, a stark contrast to the lavish bedrooms of the owners of the house.

10 Woodland Walks

The estate's woods and parkland are lovely to explore. Visitors can enjoy the exuberant birdlife and, in spring, wander through expanses of bluebells and daffodils.

Grand set table in the dining room

EDEN PROJECT

D4 Bodelva, Cornwall Hours vary, check website
edenproject.com

Occupying the site of a former china clay pit, the Eden Project's giant conservatories and extensive outdoor planting provide an innovative exploration of the plant world and human interaction with it. While it's a popular tourist attraction, the site also has a serious agenda, warning of the fragility of Earth's ecosystem through talks and workshops.

1 Visitor Centre

Adorned with sculptures, including Heather Jansch's *Driftwood Horse* (2002) made from driftwood and cork, the visitor centre's viewpoint at the top of the pit offers a taste of the marvels to come. From here, the full scale of the complex becomes apparent.

Exploring the Mediterranean Biome

2 The Core

The message of the Eden Project – humanity's dependence on Earth's resources – is presented with flair at the Core education centre and exhibition venue. The building's design mimics a tree, with Peter Randall-Page's granite sculpture, *Seed* (2007), its centrepiece.

3 Spiral Garden

This innovative garden, designed with children in mind, explores patterns in nature. Visitors can touch the plants, roll on the grass and clamber through tunnels.

4 Mediterranean Biome

The smaller of the two indoor biomes has plants from South Africa, the Mediterranean and California, US. Exhibits include orange trees, olives and bougainvillea.

TOP TIP

The site has mobility vehicles, including wheelchairs and mobility scooters.

The Eden Project's huge biomes

FACTS AND FIGURES

Nearly 60 m (200 ft) deep, the former clay pit required 85,000 tonnes of soil to turn it into a horticultural wonderland. The site contains over a million plants of more than 5,000 species. Based on architect R B Fuller's designs, Eden's massive biomes are the largest conservatories in the world – the 50-m- (164-ft-) high Rainforest Biome could hold the Tower of London.

5 Rainforest Biome

Hot and steamy, and home to a gushing waterfall, this lush biome re-creates a tropical climate for plants from West Africa, Amazonia and Malaysia.

6 Canopy Walkway

Set high above the treetops in the Rainforest Biome, this walkway gives visitors a breath-taking bird's-eye view, with the stunning biodiversity chandelier glittering overhead.

7 Outside Biome

In this roofless biome, plants are cultivated in Cornwall's temperate climate. Native Cornish flora is found alongside plants from Australasia and Chile.

8 Eden's Restaurants

The award-winning restaurants here offer globally-inspired cuisine prepared with locally sourced ingredients. There is catering for various diets as well as children's meals and Cornish cream teas. The site is also home to a range of cafés, including the Eden Coffee House and the Biome Coffee Station.

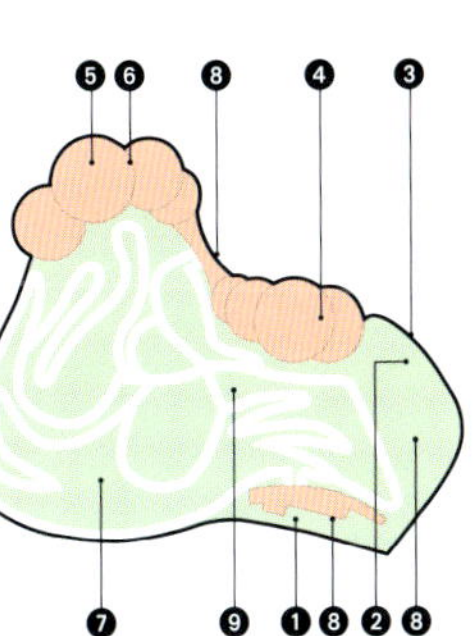

Eden Project Site Plan

9 Eden's Artworks

The artworks at the Eden Project include specially commissioned temporary exhibits, as well as permanent displays, such as a giant bee, and the dancing Dionysian figures set within the Mediterranean Biome.

10 Eden Sessions

The popular "Eden Sessions", held in summer, have included memorable gigs by stars such as the Pet Shop Boys, Elton John and Massive Attack, plus various lesser-known artists.

3

FALMOUTH AND THE FAL ESTUARY

C5

A vibrant university town and port, Falmouth owes its existence to having the world's third-largest deep harbour. Its multihued Georgian and Victorian homes spill down hillsides, while the main street follows the river, its waters visible through many a café window. Artists, students and surfers help make this the liveliest of Cornwall's towns, with a year-round calendar of festivals.

1 Falmouth Docks

C1

For centuries, this has been the last port of call for boats crossing the Atlantic, including solo navigators such as Ellen MacArthur. Used by naval ships, cruise liners and commercial vessels, it is best seen from a viewing point below Pendennis Castle.

2 National Maritime Museum, Cornwall

This museum *(p48)* focuses on the maritime history of Cornwall and the social impact of the sea on those whose lives have depended on it. Boats range from a fine 19th-century canoe built for the Duke and Duchess of Bedford to international racing yachts.

EAT

While Falmouth is home to plenty of excellent restaurants, the best place for seafood and shellfish is Beach House Falmouth *(p85)*.

3 Pendennis Castle

Built by Henry VIII in 1540–42 as one of a chain of coastal fortresses, this castle *(p46)* was designed to protect the south coast.

4 Gyllyngvase Beach

B2

Falmouth's most popular beach is a sandy crescent with rock pools at low tide. Gylly Beach Café *(p85)* and watersports add to the appeal.

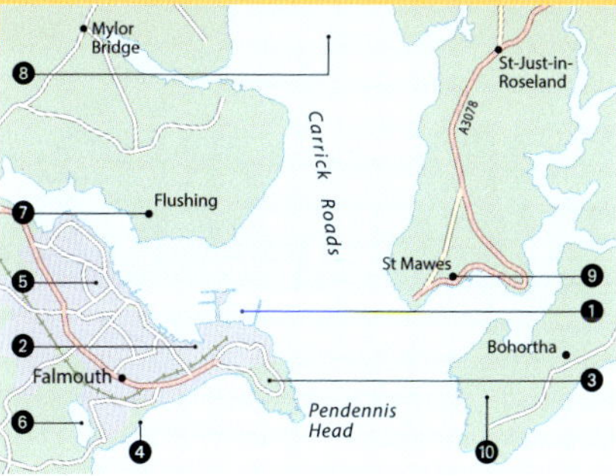

FAL OYSTERS

The Fal river is the only place in Europe where wild oysters are harvested by a fleet of sailing boats. Harvesting oysters entails dragging a metal dredge along the silty seabed and scraping the oysters into a net. Oyster fishing is strictly regulated and takes place only between 1 October and 31 March every year.

5 Falmouth Art Gallery

This small gallery *(p49)* has an outstanding permanent collection, including Pre-Raphaelite paintings, beautiful engravings of Cornish landscapes by Turner and children's illustrations. Its rotating exhibitions also showcase the work of contemporary artists.

6 Swanpool Beach and Nature Reserve

C5

A sand and shingle beach, Swanpool offers a small beach café and a scenic walk to Maenporth along the South West Coast Path. Its nature reserve is a haven for swans.

7 Flushing

C5 10 km (6 miles) from Falmouth

Originally called Nankersey, this village was renamed in the 17th century by Dutch engineers who built the piers. There are lovely riverside walks, two cosy pubs and a seafood restaurant.

8 Carrick Roads Estuary

C5 10 km (6 miles) from Falmouth

This estuary is one of the world's largest natural harbours, connecting the Fal River to the English Channel. Come for sandy coves and coastal walks.

9 St Mawes

C5 5 km (3 miles) by ferry from Falmouth

Set in a sheltered corner of the Fal Estuary, and dominated by a castle, this whitewashed village has been an exclusive holiday retreat since Edwardian times.

10 Roseland Peninsula

A long, broad peninsula *(p59)* stretching south of Truro to the banks of the Fal Estuary, the Roseland peninsula has lush hills, subtropical gardens and unspoiled sandy coves.

Bustling harbour at Fal Estuary

4

PORTHCURNO AND THE MINACK THEATRE

A6

Set between cliffs on the southern coast of the Penwith Peninsula, Porthcurno Bay is one of Cornwall's gems. Its quiet village is within easy reach of the open-air Minack Theatre, a magical place to take in some culture. This cliffside amphitheatre overlooks a sandy beach, with coastal paths on either side offering breathtaking sea views.

1 Porthcurno Beach

Porthcurno's beach *(p56)* is among the finest on the Penwith Peninsula. Sheltered by cliffs on either side, the white sand is mixed with tiny shell fragments. Coastal paths lead to Porth Chapel and Pedn Vounder beaches.

2 PK Porthcurno

A6 Apr–Oct: 10am–5pm Sat–Wed (Jul–Sep: daily); Nov–Mar: 10:30am–4pm Sat–Mon pkporthcurno.com

In 1870, an undersea cable was laid between North America and Porthcurno. A museum exploring the history of the global telegraph system now occupies the former terminus, set within a network of underground tunnels. There are daily talks and demonstrations.

3 Logan Rock

A6 3 km (2 miles) from Porthcurno

This 70-tonne rock stands on an outcrop on the eastern edge of Porthcurno Bay. The rock was dislodged from its place by a group of British seamen in 1824, but they were forced to restore it, following public outcry.

EAT

No spot is more panoramic for a snack than Minack Café, perched on a cliff edge within the complex. It is open only to visitors and playgoers.

4 White Pyramid, Pedn Vounder

A6

Halfway along the path to Logan Rock, visitors will come across this peculiar structure, placed here in the 1950s to mark the termination of a telegraph cable that once reached across the Channel to France.

5 Iron Age Fort, Treryn Dinas

A6 3 km (2 miles) from Porthcurno

This Iron Age promontory fort is set on a stunning headland. The few traces that can still be seen include four ramparts and the remains of stone houses within a ditch across the promontory.

6 Minack Theatre

On the steep cliffs above Porthcurno stands the region's famous amphitheatre *(p87)*, set into the rock.

Sunseekers relaxing at Porthcurno Beach

Picturesque setting of the Minack Theatre

THE BUILDING OF THE MINACK

Rowena Cade bought the Minack headland for £100. She built a house here and began organizing amateur theatre productions for friends in the 1920s. From this she developed the more ambitious idea of an open-air theatre, and in 1932 the first production, *The Tempest,* was staged. Cade continued to improve the site until her death in 1983.

In summer, visitors can attend a variety of theatrical performances.

7 Minack Theatre Exhibition Centre

A6

This exhibition centre tells the remarkable story of the creation of the Minack, which was the brainchild of Rowena Cade in the 1930s.

8 The Minack's Rockeries and Garden

A6

The rockeries and garden surrounding the theatre have become an attraction in their own right. The selection of plants – colourful succulents and hardy shrubs – is based on plans by Rowena Cade, the Minack's founder.

9 Walk to Land's End

From the Minack, a spectacular 7.6-km (4.7-mile) trail leads to Land's End *(p89)*. This fairly challenging clifftop route enjoys classic views of Cornwall's dramatic far-western coastal scenery, and passes idyllic coves like the stunning Porthchapel, Porthgwarra and Nanjizal.

10 Views from the Minack

In sunny weather, you could imagine yourself on Italy's Amalfi Coast as you take in the inspiring view from this cliffside theatre. The jagged headland forms a truly magnificent backdrop to performances, which run for 17 weeks of the year.

Flowers in the Minack's garden

ST IVES

B5 The Library, Gabriel St; stives-cornwall.co.uk

St Ives is like nowhere else in Britain: an intricate maze of lanes backing onto a bustling quayside and a quartet of sandy beaches. As well as the region's premier art gallery, the Tate St Ives, the town has smaller galleries displaying local scenes and landscapes that attest to its role as an artists' hub.

1 St Ia

B5 St Andrew's St stiveschurch.org.uk

This 15th-century parish church is dedicated to St Ia, the missionary after whom the town is probably named. Its features include a wagon roof and a 15th-century font.

2 St Ives Museum

B5 Wheal Dream Apr–Oct: 10:30am–4:30pm Mon–Fri, 10:30am–3:30pm Sat stivesmuseum.co.uk

Finding this museum in the maze of back streets is like discovering a hidden treasure chest. The quirky collection covers every aspect of local history, from geology and archaeology to farming and shipwrecks.

3 Tate St Ives

Very few British galleries *(p49)* have a setting as striking as this, overlooking Porthmeor Beach. Its entrance recalls the gasworks that once stood here. Inside, displays focus on the work of local artists.

TOP TIP

Cars can be parked at Barnoon, above the Tate or at the station.

4 Barbara Hepworth Museum and Sculpture Garden

Sculptor Barbara Hepworth was central to the mid-20th-century arts scene in St Ives. Her studio is one of the most compelling galleries in Cornwall *(p49)*, showing her abstract works. Larger pieces are displayed in the garden.

5 St Ives Society of Artists

Housed in the former Mariners' Church, the society's main gallery *(p49)* has contemporary work by its members. The Crypt Gallery below holds private exhibitions.

6 Trewyn Subtropical Gardens

B5

A quiet retreat with banana trees and other subtropical plants, this is a peaceful spot even in high season.

7 Porthminster Beach

B5

The largest of St Ives' beaches, Porthminster has space for swimming or lounging, and is very popular with sand sculptors. The famous Porthminster Beach Café *(p93)* is also here.

8 Porthmeor Beach

B5

Backed by cafés and the façade of the Tate, and with the promontory of the island at its eastern end, Porthmeor is the most accessible St Ives beach.

9 Leach Pottery

B5 Higher Stennack Hours vary, check website leachpottery.com

Britain's foremost potter, Bernard Leach (1887–1979) opened this pottery studio in 1920 to create his Japanese-inspired work.

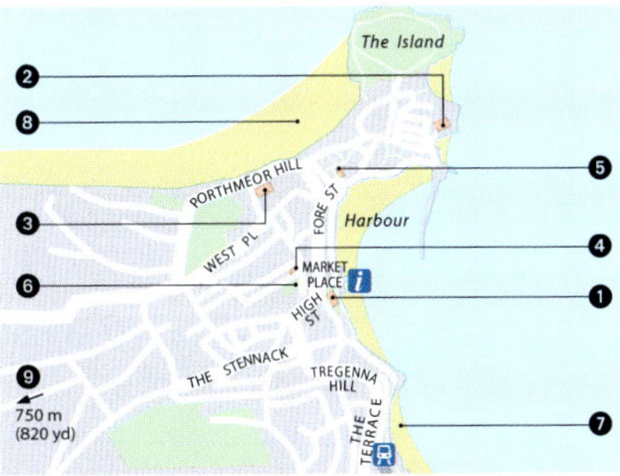

Picture-perfect St Ives and its beaches

ART IN ST IVES

In 1920, potters Bernard Leach and Shoji Hamada set up the Leach Pottery. Several artists followed, including painter Ben Nicholson and sculptor Barbara Hepworth in 1939. Along with others such as Patrick Heron and Terry Frost, they specialized in abstract work and were strongly influenced by Cornish landscapes.

10 St Ives September Festival

This boisterous, two-week festival *(p71)* features diverse events like comedy shows, tribute bands, local folk music, talks and workshops.

PENZANCE AND ST MICHAEL'S MOUNT

B5 Station Approach, Penzance; lovepenzance.co.uk

Sitting at the end of Mount's Bay, Penzance is famed for its Georgian buildings and Art Deco lido. The town also has two galleries, continuing the tradition of the colony of artists who settled in nearby Newlyn. Across the bay, St Michael's Mount is linked to the mainland by a causeway at low tide. It was granted to Benedictine monks from Mont-St-Michel, Normandy, by Edward the Confessor in the 11th century.

Impressive Egyptian House, Chapel Street

1 Market Jew Street

B5

Penzance's main street derives its name from the Cornish "Marghas Yow", meaning Thursday Market. At its top is the domed Market House.

2 Chapel Street

B5

Chapel Street has some of Penzance's comeliest buildings, including the Egyptian House dating from 1830. Across the road is the Union Hotel, featuring a minstrels' gallery.

3 The Exchange

Behind its glass façade, the town's old telephone exchange *(p49)* now houses the largest single exhibition space within 300 km (180 miles).

4 Penlee House

The Newlyn school of artists, who settled in the area in the late 19th century, are well represented in this Victorian gallery and museum *(p49)* set within a park. The group painted outdoors, aiming to capture the fleeting impressions of wind, sun and sea. The exhibits also reflect the town's fishing and mining heritage.

5 Jubilee Pool

B5 Promenade, Penzance jubileepool.co.uk

Located off Penzance's harbour, this lido dates back to 1935. It offers open-air, sea-water swimming for all ages during the summer and a geothermally heated pool.

6 Newlyn

Within walking distance of Penzance, Newlyn *(p90)* is a busy fishing port with a thriving early-morning fish market. Attractions include the Newlyn Art Gallery *(p49)*, which displays art pieces from the Newlyn school of artists founded by Stanhope Forbes.

St Michael's Mount rising from the sea

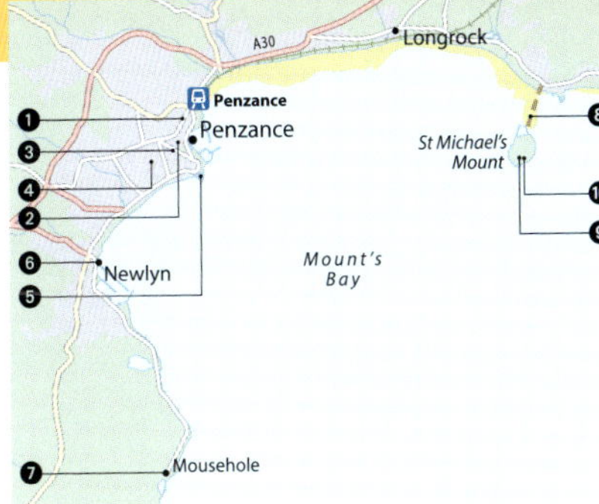

7 Mousehole

Mousehole (pronounced "mow-zel") is a village *(p88)* south of Newlyn, with tiers of whitewashed and granite cottages above a beautiful sheltered harbour.

8 The Causeway, St Michael's Mount

B5 5 km (3 miles) E of Newlyn

Set off the Marazion coast, the rocky promontory on which St Michael's Mount stands can be easily reached by boat, but at low tide visitors can walk across a causeway.

9 The Castle

B5 Marazion Apr–Oct: 10am–5pm Tue–Sun stmichaelsmount.co.uk

Originally a Benedictine priory, the castle was sold, along with the island, to John St Aubyn after the Civil War, and remains a stately family home. The Great Hall is known as the Chevy Chase Room after the frieze depicting hunting scenes described in the eponymous Scottish ballad.

10 The Chapel, St Michael's Mount

B5

From the Blue Drawing Room in the castle, a door leads into the Priory Church at the island's summit. Still regularly used for services, it has memorials to the St Aubyn family.

ST MICHAEL'S WAY

St Michael's Way *(p59)* is part of a vast European network of pilgrim routes to Santiago de Compostela in Spain. It is thought to have been used by pilgrims from Ireland and Wales who felt it safer to abandon their ships and walk across the peninsula, rather than to navigate the treacherous waters around Land's End.

7

PADSTOW

D3 South Quay; padstowlive.com

Tucked into the Camel Estuary, lively Padstow is one of Cornwall's most attractive ports, conveniently close to beaches such as Daymer, Polzeath and Trevone. Foodies know this fishing port as the domain of celebrity chef Rick Stein, who has opened several luxury hotels and seafood restaurants, which are among the best in the country.

1 Prideaux Place

On a hill above the town, this Elizabethan manor *(p53)* has been home to the Prideaux-Brune family since 1592. It features richly furnished rooms and superlative plasterwork that you can admire on a tour. Outside are formal gardens and a deer park.

2 Rick Stein's Restaurants

richstein.com

As well as the delightful Seafood Restaurant *(p79)*, Stein runs many boutique hotels, a deli, a café, a bistro, a fish-and-chip shop and a cooking school in Padstow.

3 Padstow Harbour

D3

Visitors can see the day's catch being brought in at the town's inner harbour. On the quayside is Abbey House, Padstow's oldest building.

TOP TIP

There are open-air brass-band concerts in Padstow most Sundays.

Elegantly furnished room, Prideaux Place

A busy cobblestone street in Padstow

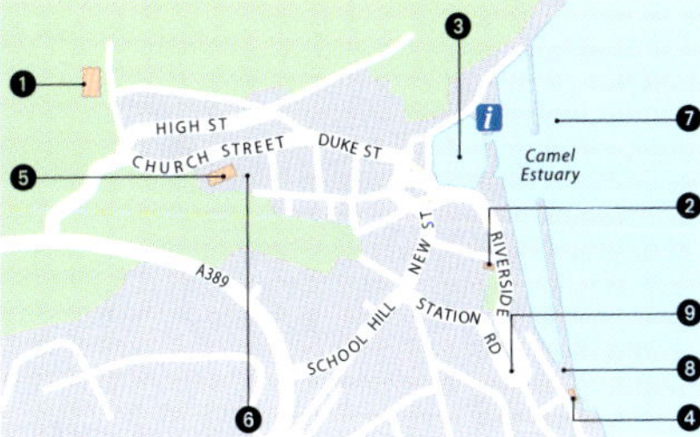

4 National Lobster Hatchery

D3 South Quay
10am–4pm daily
nationallobster hatchery.co.uk

Get close to various crustaceans at this exhibit, run by a marine charity. Tanks hold spider crabs, crayfish and sponges, as well as tiny baby lobsters.

5 St Petroc's Church

D3 Church St
01841 534898

Padstow was once known as Petrocstowe, after the missionary St Petroc, who is said to have crossed the Irish Sea on a cabbage leaf. The church is famous for the Prideaux-Brune memorial and for its magnificent 15th- or 16th-century font carved from Catacleuse stone.

6 Saints Way

Crossing the peninsula to Fowey, this 45-km (28-mile) trail *(p58)* traces the route taken by pilgrims. It follows both ancient footpaths and country lanes from its starting point at St Petroc's Church.

7 Camel Estuary

D3

The Camel, Cornwall's main north-coast river, is a haven for migrant wading birds that feed on the fertile mudflats. Passenger ferries regularly cross the estuary from Padstow to Rock.

8 Camel Trail

Cornwall's finest walking and cycling route follows a disused railway line along the River Camel for over 29 km (18 miles). You can hire bikes in Padstow *(padstowcycle hire.com)*.

9 Padstow Museum

D3 Market Place
Mid-Feb–mid-Dec: 10:30am–4pm Mon–Fri
padstowmuseum.co.uk

Housed in the old station building, this fascinating museum is packed with archaeological items, nautical models, old photos and an Obby Oss costume.

10 Obby Oss

One of Cornwall's most flamboyant festivals *(p70)* takes place annually on May Day, usually May 1. It involves two separate processions making their way around the town, led by the costumed figure of the Obby Oss.

THE OBBY OSS TALE

The festival's origins are now lost but it includes elements of other May Day festivities. Controlled by club-wielding "Teazers", the Obby Oss figures, in twirling hooped gowns, are intended to drive winter away, while the white-clothed escorts represent spring. The festivities begin the night before, when Blue Ribbon Oss leaves the Golden Lion pub.

8

DARTMOOR

J4

Southern England's greatest expanse of wilderness holds a unique fascination – its heather-strewn slopes and rocky tors are haunted by legends and scattered with 3,000-year-old relics. Hemmed in by the moorland – which offers plenty of opportunities for cycling, horse riding, caving, canoeing and climbing – are some of Devon's grandest mansions and prettiest villages.

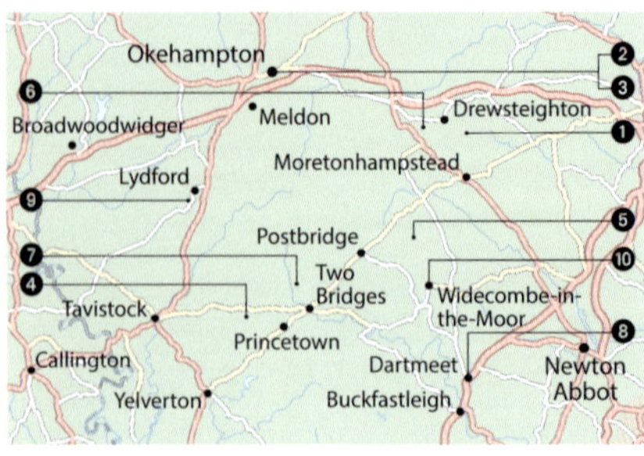

1 Fingle Bridge

J4

This bridge over the River Teign has scenic paths that weave along the shaded banks. The charming Fingle Bridge Inn (*finglebridgeinn.co.uk*) offers welcome drinks and snacks with views of the old bridge.

2 Okehampton Castle

A seemingly tottering, tall tower greets visitors as they approach this ancient Norman construction (*p46*), surrounded by woodland. Inside the castle, you can view the remains of the gatehouse, the keep and the Great Hall. Note, access is available through special events and guided tours on select days, which can be booked online. Check the website for details.

3 Museum of Dartmoor Life

Set in a cobbled courtyard in Okehampton, this museum (*p48*) provides a fascinating insight into the lives of the moor's inhabitants,

The dramatic ruins of Okehampton Castle

past and present. Displays spanning 5,000 years of life on Dartmoor include everything from antique agricultural tools and farm pick-ups to a Bronze Age hut and domestic bric-a-brac from over the years.

4 Merrivale Rows

H4

Dotted across moorland west of Princetown, these stones give an idea of the kind of prehistoric society that lived here. The complex includes huts and granite tombs.

5 Grimspound

J4 W english-heritage.org.uk

To the north of Widecombe, these circular prehistoric huts, surrounded by a thick wall, are thought to have been the inspiration for the Bronze Age village where Sherlock Holmes camped in Sir Arthur Conan Doyle's famous novel *The Hound of the Baskervilles*.

6 Castle Drogo

Said to be the last castle built in England, this formidable building *(p46)* was constructed in the early 20th century by architect Edwin Lutyens on the whim of grocery magnate Julius Drewe. The grounds lead down to the River Teign.

7 Wistman's Wood

J4

A couple of miles from the road, close to Two Bridges, this ancient, tangled wood is a remnant from the time when the moor was completely forested. It is known for its fragile mosses, and is home to the rare Horsehair lichen.

8 Dartmeet

This is a renowned beauty spot *(p59)* at the junction of the East and West Dart rivers. Nearby is one of Dartmoor's ancient crossing points, the famous clapper bridges.

9 Lydford Gorge

In this remote ravine *(p102)*, the River Lyd tumbles over the 30-m (100-ft) White Lady Waterfall and through dense vegetation that shelters wildlife.

10 Widecombe-in-the-Moor

J4 W widecombe-in-the-moor.com

This idyllic village is best known for its pinnacled church tower, a prominent local landmark, and for the famous folk ditty, "Widecombe Fair".

THE HOUND OF THE BASKERVILLES

This Conan Doyle tale has various possible sources. Local legends tell of a hunter who terrorized the Devon countryside while accompanied by a pack of red-eyed hounds. Another inspiration may be the legend of the Black Dog of Dartmoor, said to chase late-night travellers all the way to their destination.

VIEW

Enjoy classic moorland views from the top of Haytor Rocks, a granite tor located 5 km (3 miles) east of Widecombe-in-the-Moor.

St Pancras Church, Widecombe-in-the-Moor

9

EXETER

Q2 visitexeter.com

Rising up from the River Exe and dominated by the twin towers of its cathedral, Exeter holds more historical interest than any other city in the region. It has a vibrant cultural life, thanks in part to its university students and the Royal Albert Memorial Museum, as well as many restaurants and historic pubs.

1 The Quay

P3 River Exe

At one time a hardworking harbour, the Quay now offers peace and quiet by day, with its low-key cafés and crafts and antiques shops. In contrast, evenings can be lively, with pubs and clubs drawing in the crowds.

2 Exeter Cathedral

Q2 Cathedral Close 9:15am–5pm Mon–Sat, 11:30am–3pm Sun exeter-cathedral.org.uk

This 14th-century Gothic cathedral's most compelling features are its carved, honey-coloured façade and a vaulted nave.

3 Custom House

P3 Exeter Quay

This beautifully restored 17th-century building houses a visitor centre with models, paintings and an audiovisual exhibition on the city's history.

4 The Guildhall

P2 High St 01392 665500

Dating from 1330, the Guildhall still serves municipal functions, but visitors can pop in to admire the portraits in the grand main chamber.

5 St Nicholas Priory

P2 Mint Lane 10am–4pm Sun & Mon nicholaspriory.com

This Benedictine priory survived the Dissolution

Exeter skyline with its cathedral

of the Monasteries and today displays Tudor household items.

6 Royal Albert Memorial Museum

As well as its fine art collection, this splendid Victorian Neo-Gothic building *(p48)* contains a number of evocative displays. Learn about world cultures, local and natural history and gaze at beautiful textiles.

7 Underground Passages

Q2 2 Paris St
01392 665887
11am–4pm Thu, Fri & Sun, 10:30am–4:30pm Sat

This subterranean network was built in the 14th century to carry water into the city. Guided tours through the tunnels are fascinating.

8 Stepcote Hill

P3 1 km (half a mile) from the city centre

This steeply sloped medieval lane was once a main thoroughfare. At the bottom, Tudor buildings stand alongside one of Exeter's oldest churches, St Mary Steps.

9 Bill Douglas Cinema Museum

N1 Old Library, Prince of Wales Rd
10am–5pm daily
bdcmuseum.org.uk

Cinematic memorabilia is displayed in this centre on the university campus. Displays range from magic lantern slides to Charlie Chaplin posters and money boxes shaped like E.T., the alien.

EXETER'S FESTIVALS

Exeter is beloved for its festivals. At the end of May, the Exeter Fest brings live music and street food to Northernhay Gardens, while the Let's Rock Retro Festival in July sees stars perform at Powderham Castle. Meanwhile, the Exeter Respect Festival held in June and the Exeter Craft Festival in July feature local artwork.

10 Along the Exe

Enjoy a tranquil walk or cycle along the Exeter Ship Canal and the scenic Exe Estuary, and spot a range of birdlife along the way. Bikes can be hired from the Quay.

Clockwise from right **Ammonite in the Royal Albert Memorial Museum; Tudor-style bedroom, St Nicholas Priory; exploring Exeter's underground passages and tunnels; Stepcote Hill**

Exeter Cathedral

Rib-vaulted Gothic ceiling of the cathedral

1. Gothic Façade

Apostles, prophets and soldiers jostle for space on the crowded carved West Front of the cathedral. Look out for depictions of the kings Alfred, Athelstan, Canute, William I and Richard II, too.

2. Ceiling

This is the longest unbroken Gothic ceiling in the world. It makes an immediate impression with a dense network of rib-vaulting, shafts and mouldings. One of the ceiling bosses illustrates the murder in 1170 of Thomas Becket, Archbishop of Canterbury.

3. Choir

Dominated by an 18-m (60-ft) bishop's throne and a massive organ case, the Choir (or "Quire") holds stalls from the 19th century. These feature a series of carvings dating from as far back as the 1250s.

4. Cathedral Close

The lawns surrounding the cathedral are overlooked by an array of historical buildings, including the Elizabethan Mol's Coffee House, which is now a leather-goods shop.

5. Sepulchre of Hugh Courtenay

The cathedral is crammed with tombs, none more eye-catching than the 14th-century sepulchre of Hugh Courtenay, Earl of Devon, and his wife. Their tomb is carved with graceful swans and a lion.

6. Exeter Clock

The clock in the cathedral's left transept dates from the late 15th century. It features the sun and moon revolving around the Earth, in the form of a golden ball.

7. Chapter House

From the right transept, a door leads into the Chapter House, originally constructed in the 1220s but mostly rebuilt after a fire in 1413. Beneath the fine timber ceiling stands an array of sculptures from the 20th century. The Chapter House also serves as a popular venue for classical-music concerts. Pick up a leaflet for details.

8. Plaque to R D Blackmore

Among the tombs and memorials that line the walls of the aisles, one near the door is dedicated to R D Blackmore *(p50)*, the 19th-century author of the rip-roaring Exmoor romance *Lorna Doone*.

9. The Towers

Dating from the 12th century, the two central towers represent the oldest part of the cathedral. They remain the most conspicuous feature of Exeter's skyline.

10. Minstrels' Gallery

High up on the left of the nave a minstrels' gallery from 1350 depicts angels playing musical instruments.

EXETER'S HISTORY

Previously a settlement of the Celtic Dumnonii tribe, Exeter became the most westerly outpost of the Roman Empire in Britain when it was garrisoned in around 50–55 CE. Saxon settlement was followed by Danish attacks, but conditions were peaceful under the Norman regime after 1068. The town's position on the River Exe allowed it to become a major outlet for wool shipments. During the Civil War, it became the western headquarters of the Royalists and sheltered Queen Henrietta Maria. In the early 20th century, bombing during World War II spared the cathedral, but devastated the historic centre. However, the founding of the University of Exeter in 1955 helped inject new energy into the city, and the Princesshay development (the city's large shopping precinct) has since reversed some of the damage done by shabby postwar reconstruction.

TOP 10
KEY EVENTS IN EXETER'S HISTORY

1. Exeter was fortified by the Romans in 50–55 CE.
2. Around 878, the city was re-founded by Alfred the Great, King of Wessex.
3. In 1068, the Normans took control and expanded the wool trade.
4. The countess of Devon diverted the shipping trade to Topsham in the late 13th century.
5. The construction of Exeter Cathedral was completed in 1369.
6. In 1564–66, the Quay and the Ship Canal were constructed.
7. The city sheltered Queen Henrietta Maria in 1643, but fell to the Roundheads in 1646.
8. Trade ceased during the Napoleonic Wars (1799–1815), damaging the local textile industry.
9. World War II bombing flattened the city centre.
10. In 2020, Exeter Chiefs won the European Rugby Champion's Cup for the first time.

An early 19th-century illustration of Exeter Cathedral towering over the city of Exeter

ISLES OF SCILLY

A4–B4

This archipelago of more than 140 uninhabited and five inhabited islands, 45 km (28 miles) off the Cornish coast, has some of Europe's most enchanting vistas. Reached by ferry or plane, the Isles of Scilly offer white sandy beaches, wild moorland, idyllic harbours and beautiful gardens. Their mild climate makes them perfect for walking, sea-kayaking and swimming.

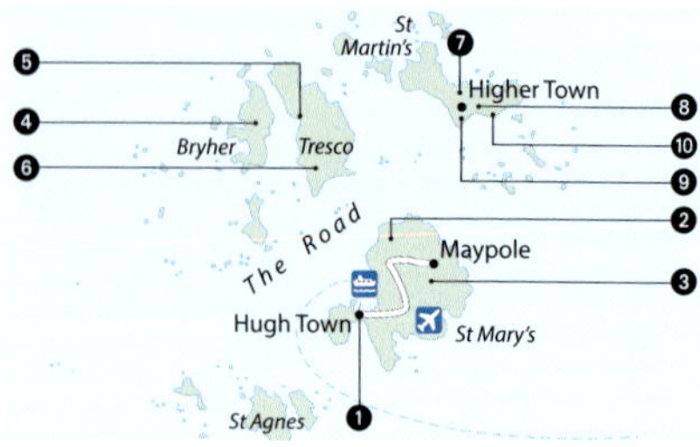

1 Isles of Scilly Cultural Centre and Museum

A4 Town Hall, Hugh Town, St Mary's Hours vary, check website iosmuseumandculturalcentre.org

Set in the Town Hall, this museum displays finds from shipwrecks, along with an array of Bronze and Iron Age artifacts.

2 Halangy Down Ancient Village

B4 St Mary's english-heritage.org.uk

A Bronze Age tomb, Bant's Carn, tops a hill above Halangy Down at St Mary's. It has been inhabited since Roman times. Excavations here have revealed 11 interconnected stone houses with thatched roofs. Visitors can hire carts (*scillycarts.com*) to travel around St Mary's.

3 HolyVale Vineyard

B4 Star Castle Hotel, St Mary's Apr–Sep: noon–4:30pm Mon–Fri star-castle.co.uk/holyvale-vineyard

This vineyard of pinot noir, chardonnay and pinot gris vines had its first vintage in 2014. It offers tours and wine tastings with canapés.

CASTLES

1 Berry Pomeroy Castle

K5 Totnes Apr–Sep: 10am–5pm daily; Oct: 10am–4pm daily english-heritage.org.uk

This romantic ruin on the edge of a wooded ravine is reputed to be haunted. Built by the Pomeroy family in the 15th century, the castle was abandoned 200 years later.

2 Restormel Castle

Still belonging to the Duchy of Cornwall, this perfectly circular Norman castle *(p84)* occupies a spur overlooking the River Fowey. In medieval terms, it was a luxury residence, with unusual facilities including running water that was piped up under pressure from a natural spring. It is now a ruin, but it is still possible to walk around its walls.

3 Pendennis Castle

C5 Castle Drive, Falmouth englishheritage.org.uk

The most westerly of the artillery forts built under Henry VIII, Pendennis and its twin St Mawes were built to safeguard the port of Falmouth, the "key to Cornwall". The castle's ramparts and bastions were erected around 1600 and the gun batteries were added during the Napoleonic wars.

Dramatic coastal setting of St Mawes Castle

4 Caerhays Castle

John Nash – architect of Buckingham Palace – designed this fantasy-Gothic structure *(p84)* in 1810. Visitors can tour the castle, but the real showpiece is the garden, with its magnolias and rhododendrons.

5 Castle Drogo

J4 Drewsteignton Hours vary, check website nationaltrust.org.uk

Designed in the 20th century by architect Edwin Lutyens, this fortress in the Teign Valley was built to resemble a medieval stronghold. Granite walls and a warren of stone corridors give it a spartan feel.

6 Okehampton Castle

H3 Okehampton english-heritage.org.uk

This Norman castle on a spur above the River Okement is a dramatic sight, dominated by the remains of its keep. The fortress, once owned by the Courtenay family – later earls of Devon – was mainly used as a hunting lodge.

7 Tintagel Castle

Set on a promontory above the turbulent Atlantic, the forlorn ruins of Tintagel *(p74)* – reached through a footbridge – resemble a fairy-tale castle.

Fortified keep at Launceston Castle

8 Launceston Castle

F3 Launceston
Apr–Sep: 10am–5pm Wed–Mon; Oct: 10am–4pm Wed–Mon
english-heritage.org.uk

A motte-and-bailey castle built shortly after the Norman Conquest, Launceston became the power centre from which the earls of Cornwall kept control of their vast estates. King Charles III was proclaimed Duke of Cornwall here in 1973.

9 Totnes Castle

K5 Totnes Apr–Sep: 10am–5pm daily; Oct: 10am–4pm daily english-heritage.org.uk

Towering above the centre of Totnes, this classic Norman construction was erected after the Conquest to dominate the Saxon town. The stone keep was added 300 years later.

10 St Mawes Castle

The most elaborately decorated of Henry VIII's coastal fortresses, this castle *(p84)* follows a clover-leaf design, with round walls that were intended to deflect enemy fire. However, the castle was never tested in war – it surrendered to Parliamentarian forces in 1646 without putting up a fight. Visitors can tour the gun rooms, governor's quarters, barracks, oubliette and kitchen.

TOP 10 ARTHURIAN SITES

1. Tintagel Castle
The most evocative of all Arthurian sights is the castle *(p74)* that is believed to be the legendary king's birthplace.

2. Slaughterbridge
E3
This spot on Bodmin Moor is said to be the site of King Arthur's last battle, against his nephew Mordred.

3. Dozmary Pool
E3
It is said that Arthur's famous sword, Excalibur, was thrown here after his final battle and was received by the Lady of the Lake.

4. The Tristan Stone
E4
This monument marks the grave of Drustanus, identified with Tristan (or Tristram), one of Arthur's knights.

5. Lyonnesse
A6
A fabled land sunk beneath the waves, Lyonnesse is another one of the candidates for Arthur's birthplace.

6. Loe Pool
B6
Like Dozmary Pool, this is a site where Excalibur was believed to have been restored to the Lady of the Lake.

7. Camelford
E3
This town on Bodmin Moor is one of several places identified with Camelot, Arthur's mythic court.

8. Castle Dore
An Iron Age hillfort *(p84)* said to have been King Mark of Cornwall's home.

9. Boscastle
After his last battle, Arthur's body was supposedly transported here *(p76)*.

10. Castle an Dinas
D4
This hillfort outside St Columb Major is believed to be Arthur's hunting lodge.

MUSEUMS

1 National Maritime Museum, Cornwall

C5 Discovery Quay, Falmouth 10am–5pm daily nmmc.co.uk

This museum displays boats from around the world, nautical equipment, interactive displays and marine art.

2 Overbeck's Garden

Scientist Otto Overbeck lived in this house *(p104)* until 1937. The garden has breathtaking views of the sea beyond, and an impressive array of plants.

3 National Marine Aquarium

Q6 Coxside, Plymouth 10am–5pm daily (last adm: 4pm) national-aquarium.co.uk

Part traditional aquarium and part 21st-century museum, this complex presents an awe-inspiring survey of ocean life, with over 50 live exhibits.

4 Royal Albert Memorial Museum

P2 Queen St 10:30am–5pm Tue, 10am–5pm Wed–Sun rammuseum.org.uk

Among the displays at Exeter's largest museum are the clocks and silverware for which the city was well-known. Sladen's study has one of the largest collections of starfish and sea urchins in the world.

5 Cornwall Museum & Art Gallery

Cornwall's county museum *(p81)* covers local geology and culture with collections of insects alongside Roman coins. Buddhist figures from Myanmar (Burma) and an unwrapped Egyptian mummy are also on display.

6 Museum of Barnstaple and North Devon

The perfect place to learn about North Devon's history, this museum *(p95)* features exhibits such as locally minted Saxon coins, a 17th-century kiln and local pottery. Natural history is well represented, too.

7 Museum of Dartmoor Life

H3 3 West St, Okehampton Mid-Mar–Oct: 10am–4pm Mon–Sat dartmoorlife.org.uk

Housed in a former mill, the Museum of Dartmoor Life illustrates aspects of the moor and its inhabitants.

Sailing crafts at the National Maritime Museum, Cornwall

8 Fairlynch Museum

Fossils, prehistoric flints, 18th-century costumes, and a range of lace and toys help to create a picture of life in South Devon through the ages. The museum building *(p104)* is fascinating in itself – a *cottage orné* (decorative cottage) built by a local shipowner.

9 Museum of Cornish Life

B5 Market Place, Helston
10am–4pm Mon–Sat
museumofcornishlife.co.uk

Dedicated to the social history of Helston and the Lizard Peninsula, this museum has sections devoted to local costume, telegraphy pioneer Guglielmo Marconi and Helston-born boxing champion Bob Fitzsimmons (1863–1917).

10 Museum of Witchcraft and Magic

E2 The Harbour, Boscastle
Apr–Oct: 10am–5:30pm daily (last adm: 4:30pm) museumofwitchcraftandmagic.co.uk

This museum houses everything there is to know about witchcraft and Europe's relationship with magic, including the history of local folk magic.

Wiccan Wheel of the Year, Museum of Witchcraft and Magic

TOP 10

ART GALLERIES

1. Penlee House
B5 Morrab Rd, Penzance
penleehouse.org.uk
This is the best place to see works by the Newlyn School artists' colony.

2. The Exchange
B5 Princes St, Penzance
01736 363715
The Exchange puts on a range of inspiring contemporary art shows.

3. Newlyn Art Gallery
A5 New Rd, Newlyn
newlynartgallery.co.uk
Exhibitions with a focus on painting and drawing.

4. The Burton at Bideford
Paintings and prized local slipware are exhibited here *(p96)*.

5. Barbara Hepworth Museum and Sculpture Garden
B5 Barnoon Hill
tate.org.uk
View sculptures exhibited in Hepworth's former St Ives studio and in her beautiful walled garden.

6. St Ives Society of Artists
B5 Norway Square
stisa.co.uk
This private gallery shows rotating exhibitions by local artists.

7. Cornwall Museum & Art Gallery
This museum *(p81)* hosts exhibitions, often with a Cornish connection.

8. Falmouth Art Gallery
C5 The Moor
falmouthartgallery.com
An eclectic collection of over 2,000 works by artists with links to Cornwall.

9. Tate St Ives
B5 Porthmeor Beach
tate.org.uk
This is a superb collection of works by well-known 20th-century and contemporary artists.

10. Exeter Phoenix
P2 Gandy St
exeterphoenix.org.uk
Exeter Phoenix includes three galleries hosting local and contemporary art shows.

WRITERS

Portrait of English novelist D H Lawrence

1 D H Lawrence

Accompanied by his wife, Frieda, D H Lawrence (1885–1930) spent the years 1915–17 in the remote village of Zennor. He loved the "high shaggy moor hills, and big sweep of lovely sea", but was forced to leave in the face of hostility. His life in Cornwall inspired Helen Dunmore's prize-winning novel, *Zennor in Darkness* (1993).

2 Henry Williamson

This novelist and naturalist (1895–1977) set his classic animal tale *Tarka the Otter* in the lush countryside of North Devon. The book has been the inspiration for the Tarka Trail *(p96)*, a recreational route around the Taw and Torridge rivers.

3 Charles Causley

Along with John Betjeman, Causley (1917–2003) is one of the best-known 20th-century poets associated with Cornwall. He was born and raised in Launceston, returning to live there in 1946. His work drew on hymns and ballads, and described Cornish life and local legends.

4 Michael Morpurgo

The Isles of Scilly – where children's writer Michael Morpurgo (b 1943) has spent many holidays writing on the island of Bryher – has inspired many of his novels, including *Why the Whales Came*, *The Wreck of the Zanzibar* and *Listen to the Moon*.

5 Winston Graham

All 12 of Graham's (1908–2003) *Poldark* novels that were written between 1945 and 2002 were set mainly around Perranporth, but also took in other parts of Cornwall, including Mousehole and Lanhydrock. The books have enjoyed great success as TV adaptations.

6 R D Blackmore

Although he wrote a number of novels, Blackmore (1825–1900) is best remembered today for his swashbuckling romance *Lorna Doone* (1869), set on Exmoor in the 17th century. Fans can visit the novel's locations, including the Valley of the Rocks outside Lynmouth.

7 Sir Arthur Conan Doyle

Dartmoor *(p36)* inspired Conan Doyle's (1859–1930) *The Hound of the Baskervilles*. It's based on local legends about black dogs that inhabited remote parts of the moor.

Famous British writer Sir Arthur Conan Doyle

Popular crime writer Agatha Christie at Greenway

8 Agatha Christie

Born in Torquay, the "Mistress of Murder" (1890–1976) spent much of her life in South Devon, particularly at Greenway *(p106)*, a grand mansion overlooking the River Dart. The settings of her country-house whodunnits give a strong flavour of the area.

9 Kenneth Grahame

Kenneth Grahame (1859–1932) regularly took breaks in Cornwall, and began writing *The Wind in the Willows* as letters to his young son while staying at the Greenbank Hotel in Falmouth. A boat trip along the River Fowey inspired the opening scene, where Ratty and Mole make a trip along the river for a picnic.

10 Daphne du Maurier

Having spent many childhood holidays in Cornwall, du Maurier (1907–89) eventually settled outside Fowey. Drawn to Cornwall's secluded creeks and the wild romance of the moors, she set some of her novels here – including *Rebecca* and *Jamaica Inn*. An arts festival in Fowey *(p70)* celebrates her work.

TOP 10 FILMING LOCATIONS

1. Bodmin Moor

The BBC's popular TV series *Poldark* (2015–2019), was based and filmed in the Cornwall area, notably on Bodmin Moor *(p76)*.

2. Dartmoor

Dartmoor *(p36)* provided the backdrop for *War Horse* (2011) and *The Hounds of Baskerville* episode of the 2012 BBC mini-series *Sherlock*.

3. Saunton Sands

This beach *(p98)* has been the location for many films and TV series including *A Very English Scandal* (2018).

4. Teignmouth

K4

The harbour here has been the location for a part of the film, *The Mercy* (2018), starring Colin Firth.

5. Saltram House

Plymouth's Saltram House *(p53)* was featured in a film adaptation of Jane Austen's *Sense and Sensibility* (1995).

6. Hartland Abbey

The TV series *The Night Manager* (2016) was filmed here *(p52)*.

7. Charlestown

D4

This port town's harbour can be seen in *Poldark*, the *Pirates of the Caribbean* films and more.

8. Antony House

H5 Ferry Ln, Torpoint

nationaltrust.org.uk

This 18th-century home was used when filming *Alice in Wonderland* (2008).

9. Caerhays Castle

Miss Peregrine's Home for Peculiar Children (2016) used this castle and estate as a backdrop setting *(p84)*.

10. St Michael's Mount

This picturesque tidal island *(p32)* became Driftmark, home of House Velaryon, in the TV series *House of the Dragon* (2022–). The show shot scenes in a number of other places around Cornwall, including Holywell Bay.

HOUSES

1 Hartland Abbey

G2 Hartland, Bideford House: Apr–Sep: 2–5pm Sun–Thu; gardens: Apr–Sep: 11am–5pm Sun–Thu hartlandabbey.com

Founded in 1157, this was the last English abbey to be dissolved by Henry VIII. A private home ever since, its decor and architecture are magnificent. Highlights are the vaulted Alhambra Corridor and the Regency library with Gainsborough and Reynolds portraits.

2 Knightshayes Court

K3 Bolham, Tiverton House: Mar–Oct: 11am–4pm daily; gardens: 10am–5pm daily (Nov–Feb: to 4pm) nationaltrust.org.uk

The original designer of this Victorian country pile was William Burges. Later, Burges was fired, but enough of his elaborate Gothic-style interiors remain in the library, vaulted hall and the arched red drawing room. From November to February, only the ground floor is open to visitors.

Victorian Gothic mansion, Knightshayes Court

3 Pencarrow

D3 Bodmin House: Apr–Oct: 11am–4pm Sun–Fri (last tour: 3pm); gardens: 10am–5pm daily pencarrow.co.uk

Accessible only via guided tour, this elegant 18th-century mansion is known for its porcelain and paintings, including portraits by English painter Joshua Reynolds. The estate is home to England's first Victorian rock garden.

4 Lanhydrock

This 17th-century palace *(p22)* was rebuilt in the High Victorian style after a fire in 1881, but the North Wing containing the Jacobean Long Gallery and the gatehouse survived. The building is filled with the accoutrements of a 19th-century mansion.

5 Buckland Abbey

Founded as a Cistercian abbey in 1278, Buckland *(p102)* was disbanded in the Dissolution of the Monasteries, converted into a private home by the distinguished mariner Richard Grenville and subsequently acquired by Francis Drake in 1580. Drake's seafaring exploits are related here and visitors can also admire the Great Barn.

Period furniture in a room, Hartland Abbey

6 St Michael's Mount

This rocky island *(p32)* was linked with Normandy's Mont-St-Michel until 1424 and later became a fortified private home. The best-preserved parts are the Chevy Chase Room, the 14th-century church and the Lady Chapel, later converted into a drawing room.

7 Prideaux Place

D3 Padstow Apr–Sep: 11am–5pm Sun–Fri

Occupied by the Prideaux family since 1592, this fine manor house contains numerous treasures, including loot from the Spanish Armada. The grounds include a classical temple, a deer park, a grotto and a 9th-century Celtic cross.

8 Cotehele House

Hidden in the byways of the Tamar Valley, this Tudor palace *(p82)* is a must for all fans of needlework, with the bedrooms adorned in tapestries – the absence of electric lights has helped to preserve them.

9 Saltram House

H5 Plympton House: Mar–Oct: 11am–4:30pm daily, late Nov–Feb: 11am–5pm daily; gardens: 10am–5pm daily nationaltrust.org.uk

This 18th-century mansion is set in parkland, outside Plymouth. Its exterior is matched by the rooms inside, each decorated with a dazzling array of art.

10 Trerice

An architectural gem with ornate fireplaces and ceilings, this small Elizabethan manor *(p77)* has a good collection of English furniture, clocks and examples of needlework. The highlight is the barrel ceiling of its Great Chamber.

Vintage carriage clock, Trerice

TOP 10 CHURCHES, ABBEYS & CATHEDRALS

1. St Neot
E3 St Neot
saintneot.church
This 15th-century church has stained-glass windows depicting Noah's Ark and St Neot himself.

2. Truro Cathedral
Built between 1880 and 1910, this monument *(p84)* incorporates the 600-year-old parish church of St Mary's.

3. St Nonna
E3 Altarnun
This church on Bodmin Moor is famous for its 79 carved bench ends.

4. Buckfast Abbey
This complex *(p106)* was founded in the 11th century and rebuilt by Benedictine monks.

5. Exeter Cathedral
The Exeter Cathedral *(p38)*, with its twin Norman towers, is the grandest of Cornwall and Devon's churches.

6. Crediton Parish Church
The rich interior of this church *(p103)* is illuminated by large windows.

7. St Mary
L3 College Rd, Ottery St Mary otterystmary.org.uk
This 13th-century church features a 14th-century astronomical clock that still works.

8. St Just-in-Roseland
Situated on the Roseland peninsula, this church *(p84)* is surrounded by magnolias and palms.

9. St Enodoc
This tiny 13th-century church *(p78)* lies in the middle of a golf course, within sight of the Camel Estuary.

10. St Petroc's Church
D4 Bodmin
bodminchurch.com
Built around 1470, this is the largest parish church in Cornwall and has a typical Cornish wagon roof.

GARDENS

1 Lost Gardens of Heligan

There is an air of mystery about this "lost garden". First planted in the late 18th century, the garden *(p82)* was neglected to the point of decay until it was rediscovered by Tim Smit, the guiding light behind the Eden Project *(p24)*. Smit restored the garden while preserving its wild, tangled character. The site includes walled flower gardens and a sub-tropical "Jungle" valley.

2 Trelissick Garden

Sheltered by woodlands, this Cornish garden *(p82)* features rhododendrons, magnolias and acers. Bordering the River Fal, the site affords views across the Carrick Roads Estuary.

3 Trengwainton Gardens

A5 Madron, Penzance Mid-Feb–Oct: 10am–5pm Sat–Thu nationaltrust.org.uk

An abundance of trees and shrubs, sheltered walled gardens and a woodland area make this diverse garden a delight to explore. In spring, the blooming azaleas, camellias and rhododendrons add to the colourful display. Picnic by the stream or enjoy the views from the terrace.

4 Bicton Park

This extensive estate *(p104)* has formal parterres of bedding plants and a renowned collection of trees, including a giant Grecian fir. There is an elegant Palm House, dating from the 1820s, while the Tropical House features the Bicton orchid. A wood-land railway provides scenic rides through the landscaped park.

5 Tresco Abbey Garden

A4 Tresco 10am–4pm daily tresco.co.uk

First planted in 1834, these Isles of Scilly gardens have been carefully nurtured by five generations of the same family. The region's climate, the mildest in the UK, has allowed the cultivation of tropical plants from around the southern hemisphere. The Tresco Abbey ruins form an evocative backdrop.

Strolling Tresco Abbey Garden

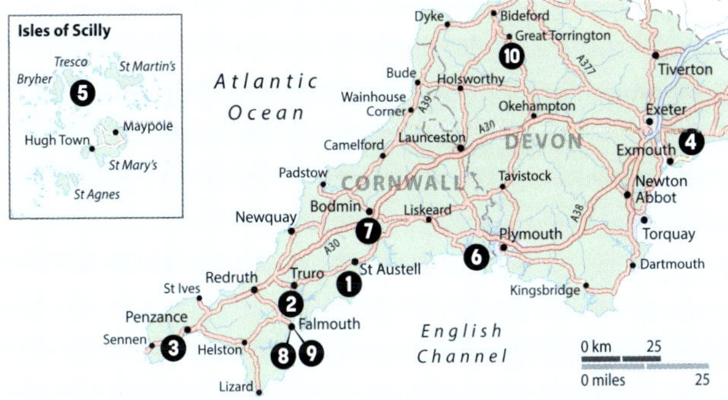

6 Mount Edgcumbe

Located on the Rame Peninsula outside Plymouth, Mount Edgcumbe *(p84)* has Italian, French and American formal gardens and is home to the national camellia collection, which flowers from January.

7 Lanhydrock

D4 Treffry Ln, Bodmin
Apr–Sep: 10:30am–5:30pm daily (Oct: to 5pm) nationaltrust.org.uk

Surrounding this grand manor house are a number of horticultural spectacles, including a yew-hedged herbaceous garden, at its best in summer. Other highlights are magnolias from Sikkim and southern China, plus hybrid rhododendrons and geraniums.

8 Trebah Garden

This subtropical garden *(p88)* features a selection of 100-year-old tree ferns and water gardens with koi carp. Plants from around the world are grown here, including gunnera (giant rhubarb) from Brazil and Australasian tree ferns. Rhododendrons and hydrangeas lead to a private beach on the River Helford.

9 Glendurgan

Set in a wooded valley on the banks of the Helford, this garden *(p90)* features walled areas and herbaceous planting with brilliant colour and foliage. The spring-flowering magnolias and camellias are especially impressive. Children will enjoy the baffling laurel maze dating from 1833 and the Giant's Stride rope swing.

10 RHS Garden Rosemoor

H2 Great Torrington
Apr–Sep: 10am–6pm daily; Oct–Mar: 10am–5pm daily (last adm: 4pm) rhs.org.uk

In North Devon's Torridge Valley, Rosemoor provides year-round interest, with snowdrops in winter, rhododendrons in spring, flower borders in summer and fiery hues in autumn. The most spectacular displays, however, are 2,000 roses with more than 200 cultivars. Woodland walks provide further interest.

Admiring rows of lettuce, RHS Garden Rosemoor

BEACHES

1 Blackpool Sands
K6

Backed by lovely woods and meadows, this family-friendly beach is an enticing sight as it swings into view on the road from Dartmouth. Its location and clear water make it one of South Devon's best swimming spots.

2 Whitesand Bay
A5

An expanse of fine sand near Land's End, this beach is a favourite with surfers and families alike. It has a beachside café, and at the more popular southern end – Sennen Cove – you'll find the Old Success Inn *(p118)*.

3 Porthcurno Beach
A6

Porthcurno is squeezed between granite cliffs. The rock-hewn Minack Theatre is located to one side and there is a museum of telegraphy at the back of the beach.

4 Par Beach, Isles of Scilly
B4

Majestic, bare and wild, the beaches on St Martin's are considered to be the best on the Isles of Scilly. Par Beach, on the island's southern shore, is probably the most impressive – a long, empty strand looking out onto rocks that make up the Eastern Isles.

5 Watergate Bay
C4

Watergate Bay is home to Wavehunters *(wavehunters.co.uk)*, which offers adventurous activities including kitesurfing and landboarding. The bay is not very sheltered, so make sure you carry some windbreakers. In the summer months there is a drive-in cinema on the cliffs above the bay.

6 Fistral Bay
C4

Surf enthusiasts flock to this beach for surfing competitions. A surf centre supplies equipment for rent. Most of the sand is covered by water at high tide, and strong currents mean that children especially need to be careful. Lifeguards are present throughout the summer.

7 Woolacombe Bay

Surfers come from far and wide to Woolacombe Bay *(p95)*, one of the West Country's most famous surfing beaches. The beach is popular with families and there is a warren of dunes behind for exploring.

Lovely Par Beach backed by dunes

8 Tunnels Beaches, Ilfracombe

H1 Bath Place, Ilfracombe
Apr & Sep: 10am–5pm daily; May–Aug: 10am–6pm daily
tunnelsbeaches.co.uk

These private beaches are named after the tunnels that have provided access to them since 1823, when the swimming was segregated by gender – they're still referred to as the "Ladies' Beach" and "Gentlemen's Beach". There is a tidal bathing pool and top-class rockpooling. One beach is often closed for weddings.

9 Croyde Bay

H1

Sandwiched between the west-facing Saunton Sands and Woolacombe, this compact bay has campsites nearby and the village has pubs and bars.

10 Kynance Cove

B6

This is one of the best options on the Lizard Peninsula, where beaches are few and far between. The ten-minute walk from the car park is worth it for the beach's fine white sands, rocky spires and surrounding grassy areas.

WALKS

Traversing a path on the Tarka Trail

1 Tarka Trail

Inspired by Henry Williamson's animal tale *Tarka the Otter* *(p96)*, this figure-of-eight route centres on Barnstaple and takes in coastal and inland areas of North Devon. If you include the section covered by the Tarka Line between Eggesford and Barnstaple, the route is 288 km (180 miles).

2 Two Moors Way/ Coast-to-Coast Walk

J1–K1

The 164-km (102-mile) Two Moors Way, which links Exmoor and Dartmoor, can be extended around 24 km (15 miles) at its southern end between Ivybridge and Wembury to make it a coast-to-coast hike. The most dramatic scenery is on Dartmoor, though Lynmouth at the northern end makes a striking end point.

3 Camel Trail

D3–D4

The Camel River flows through some of Cornwall's most beautiful landscapes, from the edge of Bodmin Moor to the sea at Padstow. A 29-km (18-mile) bike and walking trail follows a disused railway line through wooded valleys to the mudflats of the Camel Estuary.

4 Coast and Clay Trail

D4–C5

This 75-km (45-mile) network of shorter interlinked paths around Truro, St Austell and the Roseland Peninsula, is designed to give a taste of Cornish history – from gardens and fishing villages to the china clay industry and the Eden Project.

5 Saints Way

D3–E4

A coast-to-coast trail, this route covers about 48 km (30 miles) between Padstow and Fowey. There is no evidence that the whole route was used in the Middle Ages, but parts of it were certainly travelled by pilgrims.

6 Dart Valley Trail

J5–K5

Experience the Dart Valley on this 26-km (16-mile) walk, which swoops high above or runs alongside the River Dart. Half of it is a circuit, involving two ferry crossings, and the other half follows the river to Totnes.

7 Dartmoor Way

J4

This circular 175-km (109-mile) route crosses some of Dartmoor's

Admiring the view from the South West Coast Path

most thrilling and varied terrain, including rugged moorland, wooded valleys and disused railway tracks. The trail mostly skirts the edge of the moor, but connects with the 37-km (23-mile) High Moor Link, which crosses the centre of central Dartmoor.

8 East Devon Way

L4

Also known as the Foxglove Way, this undulating inland trail follows footpaths, bridleways and quiet country lanes between Exmouth and Uplyme, north of Lyme Regis over the Dorset border. It is 61 km (38 miles) long.

9 St Michael's Way

B5

Weaving between Lelant, near St Ives, and Marazion, this 19.5-km (12.5-mile) trail was once used by pilgrims and travellers to avoid the treacherous waters at Land's End.

10 South West Coast Path

K5

At 1,014 km (630 miles) in length, this is England's longest National Trail, used by anyone who walks for any distance along the Cornwall and Devon seaboard. Starting in Minehead in Somerset, and winding along the coasts of Devon, Cornwall and finally Dorset, this scenic trail is predominantly hilly and often dramatic.

TOP 10 BEAUTY SPOTS

Picturesque Golitha Falls

1. Golitha Falls, Bodmin Moor
E3
A series of waterfall cascades gush through oak and beech woodland.

2. Hartland Point
Cliffs flank this promontory *(p98)*, which offers views of Lundy Island.

3. Roseland Peninsula
C5
This is one of the region's unspoiled spots, with two waterside churches.

4. Valley of the Rocks, Exmoor
Striking rock formations and coastal views characterize this dry valley *(p98)*.

5. Lydford Gorge, Dartmoor
A lovely spot *(p102)* with riverside walks, a whirlpool and a waterfall.

6. Lizard Point
C6
A rocky promontory with invigorating walks to beaches and a lighthouse.

7. Watersmeet, Exmoor
J1
This beautiful confluence of the East Lyn and Hoar Oak rivers is a perfect spot for walks.

8. Cape Cornwall, Penwith Peninsula
A5
This craggy headland is overlooked by an abandoned tin-mine chimney stack.

9. Dartmeet, Dartmoor
J4
The West and East Dart rivers merge here, near a clapper bridge.

10. Hell Bay, Isles of Scilly
A4
This dramatic, stunning bay bears the full brunt of Atlantic storms.

TRAIN JOURNEYS

1 Looe Valley Line

E4 greatscenicrailways.co.uk

The fishing port of Looe is linked to Liskeard by this branch line dating from 1860. The route runs beside the river through the Looe Valley.

2 Launceston Steam Railway

F3 launcestonsr.co.uk

These narrow-gauge Victorian steam engines run for 4 km (2.5 miles) between Launceston and Newmills. At Launceston Station visitors can see restoration projects as well as vintage cars and motorbikes at the Transport and Engineering Museum.

Boarding the Launceston Steam Railway

3 Bodmin and Wenford Railway

D4 bodminrailway.co.uk

This railway is one of the best ways to explore the countryside around Bodmin. The terminus at Bodmin Parkway is linked by a 3-km (2-mile) path to Lanhydrock *(p22)*. There is direct access to the Camel Trail from Boscarne Junction and to Cardinham Woods from Colesloggett Halt.

4 Atlantic Coast Line

C4–D4 greatscenicrailways.co.uk

This 33-km (21-mile) coast-to-coast line runs from the English Channel at Par Station to Newquay on the Atlantic, passing through the lunar landscape of china clay country.

5 South Devon Railway

From a station outside Totnes, the steam trains of the South Devon Railway *(p106)* depart several times

LMS Royal Scot **running on the South Devon Railway**

daily, six to seven days a week from April to October. The scenic 10-km (7-mile) journey leads to Buckfastleigh, with a stop at Staverton.

6 Riviera Line

K4 greatscenicrailways.co.uk

Between Exeter and Newton Abbot, the Riviera Line runs beside two estuaries, the Exe and the Teign, offering delightful vistas over serene mudflats populated by wading birds.

7 Tarka Line

H1–H3 greatscenicrailways.co.uk

Named after *Tarka the Otter*, this 65-km (39-mile) line, centred on Barnstaple, weaves through rural Devon. After Crediton, it sticks close to the River Taw, passing through a woodland.

8 Tamar Valley Line

F4 greatscenicrailways.co.uk

The highlight of this branch line is the Calstock Viaduct between Devon and Cornwall. For those keen to enjoy a drink along the way, a "rail ale trail" is available on this and other scenic regional lines.

9 Paignton and Dartmouth Steam Railway

K5 dartmouthrailriver.co.uk

This heritage line runs from Paignton Station around the Tor Bay coast, then follows the River Dart to Kingswear. A round trip ticket includes a river cruise from Dartmouth to Totnes and the coach ride back to Paignton.

10 St Ives Bay Line

B5 greatscenicrailways.co.uk

This branch line from St Erth (a village in Cornwall) is the best way to reach St Ives *(p30)*, avoiding all the motorway traffic. It edges along the Hayle Estuary before winding around the beaches of St Ives Bay, ending up near Porthminster Beach.

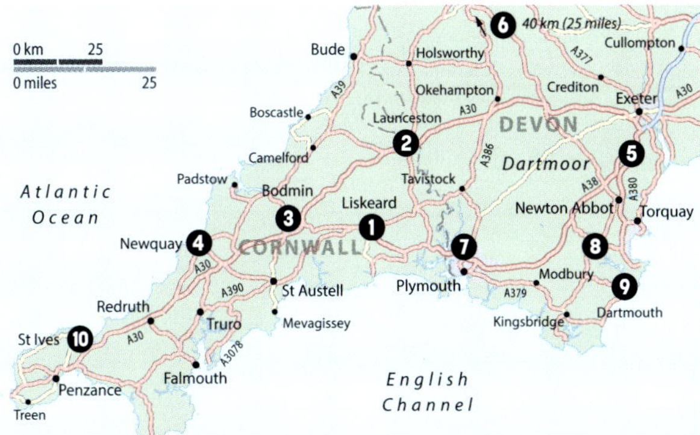

FAMILY ATTRACTIONS

1 Geevor Tin Mine

A5 Pendeen, Penzance 9am–5pm Sun–Fri geevor.com

Learn about Cornwall's mining history up close at the Geevor Tin Mine, where you can descend underground on a guided tour or explore the museum and machinery on ground level. There are hands-on exhibits and children's activities, including gem panning and an interactive coastal trail. The site also features an excellent restaurant with spectacular sea views.

2 Kents Cavern

K5 Ilsham Rd, Torquay kents-cavern.co.uk

Stone Age living is brought to life in one of the country's most significant prehistoric sites, with tours of the caves, treasure hunts, foraging trails and cave painting. There are also ghost tours and special seasonal events.

3 Babbacombe Model Village

K5 Hampton Ave, Babbacombe, Torquay Hours vary, check website model-village.co.uk

Explore a miniature world with working railways, gardens, a celebrity mansion, a naturist beach and 4D theatre as well as indoor displays at this site. After dusk, 10,000 bulbs light up its streets, homes and gardens.

4 Newquay Zoo

Cornwall's largest zoo *(p77)*, set in lakeside gardens, is home to lions, lynxes, meerkats and tortoises. Activities for kids include exploring the Tarzan Trail and the Dragon Maze.

5 Bodmin Jail

Built in 1779 from granite sourced from Bodmin Cuckoo Quarry, this spooky, atmospheric prison is now a major attraction *(p78)*. Its dark, fascinating history is brought to life through interactive displays, theatrical sound effects and storytelling. Be warned: it's not for the very young or faint-hearted. Also on site is a luxury boutique hotel, where guests can stay in converted prison cells.

6 Cornish Seal Sanctuary

This sanctuary *(p90)* rescues injured seals pup from around the Cornish coast, rehabilitates them and releases them back into the

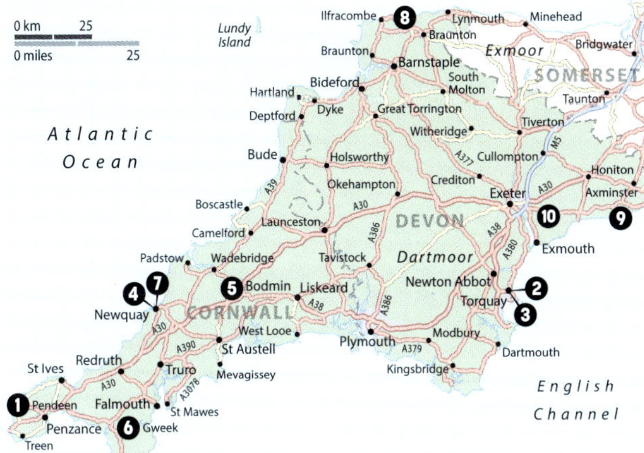

wild. It's a great place to learn about Cornish wildlife and see animal welfare in action – and meet some adorable Icelandic puffins, too.

7 Pirate's Quest Adventure Golf

C4 22 St Michael's Rd, Newquay Hours vary, check website piratesquest.co.uk

A pirate-themed experience that combines mini-golf with enthusiastic actors, special effects and superb sets to transport players back to the age of Cornish swashbuckling free-traders.

8 Watermouth Castle

H1 Berrynarbor, Ilfracombe Hours vary, check website watermouthcastle.com

This Victorian folly castle and adventure park includes a model railway, crazy golf and toboggan run. The castle itself displays suits of armour and a 1950s organ on which life-size figures play instruments.

Idyllic Babbacombe Model Village

Family-friendly ride at Crealy Theme Park & Resort

9 Pecorama

M4 Underleys, Beer, Seaton Apr–Oct: 10am–4pm Tue–Sat pecorama.co.uk

Home of the iconic model railway manufacturers Peco, Pecorama is a key attraction for children. The highlight here is a ride on the 18.5-cm- (7.25-inch-) gauge Beer Heights Light Railway – running along a mile of track with coastal views.

10 Crealy Theme Park & Resort

The award-winning Crealy Theme Park & Resort *(p103)* has more than 60 rides, plus indoor and outdoor activities, live entertainment, a farm and a small zoo.

PUBS

1 The Masons Arms

Located only 10 minutes from the beach, this East Devon inn *(p99)* serves locally brewed bitter and top-notch food, including local seafood and Exmoor beef. Try the delicious chocolate and raspberry mousse for dessert. There's outdoor seating and rooms are also available upstairs. Set menus are on offer for lunch.

2 The Sloop Inn

One of Cornwall's oldest pubs *(p92)*, with beams, benches and nooks, the Sloop is a popular St Ives haunt right on the harbour. It offers a fine range of real ales and decent pub fare. Make sure to try their signature gin; you can even take a bottle home. Punters spill out onto the cobbled harbourside in summer.

3 Ship Inn

This excellent inn *(p92)* in Mousehole stands directly above the harbour in a tiny fishing village. The Tinners and Tribute ales and fresh prawns are worth sampling. If you miss out on a seat with harbour views, sit in the tiny patio garden upstairs. Accommodation is also available.

4 Turks Head

Said to be Penzance's oldest pub, the Turks Head *(p92)* dates from 1233 and has a maze of low-ceilinged rooms, a beer garden and a smugglers' tunnel. Don't miss their hearty pies and seasonal cocktails and mocktails.

5 Blue Anchor Inn

One of the four original brew pubs remaining in England, this lovely Helston pub *(p92)* dates back to the 15th century. It's been brewing its own beer, Spingo Ale, for 600 years.

6 Prospect Inn

P3 The Quay, Exeter
theprospectexeter.co.uk

The family-friendly Prospect Inn is located right on the waterfront, with outdoor tables on the quay – perfect for watching summer sunsets. Enjoy well-cooked meals and a good selection of local beers and ciders here.

7 Blisland Inn

E3 Blisland 01208 850739

A traditional country pub on Bodmin Moor, the Blisland Inn has Toby jugs hanging from wooden beams and walls festooned with photographs. A wide variety of real ales and tasty pub food is available.

Enjoying pub grub at the Masons Arms

8 Warren House Inn

J4 4 km (2 miles)
NE of Postbridge, Dartmoor
01822 880208

The third-highest pub in England stands in solitary splendour on Dartmoor. It is a welcome sight to walkers, offering warmth and comfort with two hearths – one that has reputedly been kept burning since 1845 – and good food.

9 Bridge Inn

K4 Bridge Hill, Topsham
thebridgeinntopsham.co.uk

The pink-walled, 16th-century Bridge Inn, with its real ales and traditional trappings, is one of Devon's best pubs. It is reputedly the first pub to have been graced by Queen Elizabeth II in an official capacity, when she visited the region in 1998.

10 Tinners Arms

This historic pub *(p92)*, which dates from 1271, is where D H Lawrence stayed when he came to Zennor. The food menu consists of local produce, meat and seafood. There's a cosy log fire, and occasionally live music.

Bartender pouring a draught beer in the Tinners Arms

TOP 10 LOCAL BREWERIES

1. St Austell
D4 **staustellbrewery.co.uk**
This is one of the major brewers in Cornwall; traditional cask ales here include HSD and Tribute.

2. Harbour Brewing Company
D4 **harbourbrewing.com**
A progressive Cornish microbrewery offering a range of innovative beers.

3. Sharp's
D3 **sharpsbrewery.co.uk**
The Cornish producer of fine beers such as Doom Bar, Wolf Rock, Coaster, Atlantic, Sea Fury and Orchard.

4. Otter
L3 **otterbrewery.com**
A Honiton-based brewery which produces five regular beers and one winter ale.

5. Hanlons
K3 **hanlons-brewery.myshopify.com**
This Devon brewery produces some award-winning cask and bottled beers.

6. Country Life
H2 **countrylifebrewery.co.uk**
Bideford-based producer of ales such as Old Appledore, the light-coloured Golden Pig, and Country Bumpkin.

7. Spingo Ales
B5 **spingoales.com**
These famous brews are available only in Helston's Blue Anchor, in four distinctive varieties from 4.5 per cent to 6.5 per cent ABV.

8. Driftwood Spars Brewery
C4 **driftwoodsparsbrewery.com**
Award-winning microbrews from the Driftwood Spars brewpub at St Agnes.

9. Grampus Brewery
H1 **thegrampusinn.co.uk**
This inn has been brewing a selection of beers since 2014, and small-batch gin since 2019.

10. Skinners
C5 **skinnersbrewery.com**
This Truro-based brewery features ales named after Cornish locations and folk heroes, such as Betty Stogs.

LOCAL DISHES

Crab sandwiches, a popular lunch in Devon

1 Crab Sandwiches

While any fish or seafood dish could have a spot on this list, wild crab served between thick slices of buttered bread is a perennial favourite. A coastal staple throughout the region, crab sandwiches are especially popular in south Devon and around Newlyn.

2 Cream Tea

Without question, the simple cream tea is one of the region's most famous and beloved dishes. Along with a pot of tea, you'll be served a couple of scones, some clotted cream and some jam – an unfussy and delicious combination which showcases these rural counties' delicious farm produce. Now you just have to decide whether to spread the jam first, or the cream (each county does it differently).

3 Pasties

The phrase "Cornish pasty" has a Protected Geographical Indication, so only specific products made within the county can use that name. You'll always see a classic Cornish pasty on bakery menus – made with shortcrust pastry, crimped on the side, and filled with potato, swede, beef and onion – but bakers often get creative with other fillings, (anything from cauliflower bhaji to spiced crab). Ask around for local favourite spots, or make a beeline for St Agnes Bakery *(stagnesbakery.co.uk)*, St Ives Bakery *(stivesbakery.co.uk)* or Lavenders in Penzance *(lavenderscornishpasties.co.uk)*.

4 Cornish Yarg

The West Country offers several locally made cheeses, with standouts including mild, creamy Cornish Blue and Quicke's rich, complex clothbound cheddars. The jewel in its cheesy crown, though, is the delightfully named Cornish Yarg. Made from sheep's milk, this semi-hard cheese is wrapped in nettle leaves, adding an earthy note that complements its buttery interior.

5 Thunder and Lightning

An alternative to a cream tea, this dish is made by cutting open a Cornish split (a soft yeasted bread bun), slathering it in clotted cream, and drizzling over jagged lines of golden syrup or treacle – like slashes of lightning. It's well worth trying if you spot it on the menu.

6 Wine

With its fertile farmland and pleasant climate, the West Country has a long history as a wine-growing region, and in recent years the industry has gone from strength to strength. Well-established, award-winning wineries offering tours and tastings include Lympstone Manor *(p107)*, Camel Valley *(p76)*, Calancombe Estate *(calancombe-estate.com)* and Alder Vineyard *(aldervineyard.uk)*.

7 Saffron Cake

Fancy a sweet treat? Try a slice (or two) of this traditional Cornish fruit cake. Consisting of a rich, buttery loaf studded with sultanas and dried citrus peel, the saffron cake is made extra special with the addition of the eponymous spice, which lends it a rich flavour, delicate fragrance and lovely golden colour.

8 Ice Cream

With their dairy farming tradition and summer-holiday appeal, it's no surprise that Cornwall and Devon produce some exceptional ice cream. Along with nationally popular home-grown brands like Roskilly's *(p68)* and Callestick Farm *(p78)*, there are numerous local favourites, too – consider Moomaid of Zennor *(moomaidofzennor.com)* or Salcombe Dairy *(salcombedairy.co.uk)*.

9 Stargazy Pie

The unusual stargazy (or starry-gazy) pie gets its name from the pilchards that peek out through the crust, as though looking up at the sky. Legend has it that the dish was created in Mousehole *(p88)*, when fisherman Tom Bawcock sailed out in a storm to get food for the village's starving residents. It's traditionally eaten on 23 December to commemorate his miraculous catch.

10 Cider

From cloudy local scrumpies to golden, sparkling ciders, the West Country's classic tipple comes in every form and flavour. Pull up a bar stool at a local pub and chances are you'll find at least a couple of options on tap; better yet, head to a local brewery *(p65)*.

Bottles of local scrumpy cider on sale

TOP 10 CREAM-TEA SPOTS

1. Clock Tower Café
L4 Connaught Gardens, Sidmouth clocktowersidmouth.com
Enjoy the sea views while indulging in delicious homemade cakes.

2. Falmouth Hotel
C5 Castle Beach, Falmouth falmouthhotel.co.uk
Nibble scones on the hotel terrace.

3. Otterton Mill
Fine scones are baked and served at this ancient mill *(p104)*.

4. Charlotte's Tea House
C5 Boscowan Street, Truro charlottes-teahouse.co.uk
Generous cream teas, with gluten-free and savoury options, in a listed Victorian building.

5. Weavers Cottage Tea Garden
K5 Cockington, Torquay weaverscottage.uk
A thatched cottage where a selection of tea-time treats can be enjoyed.

6. Southern Cross
L4 Newton Poppleford, near Sidmouth southerncrossdevon.co.uk
The perfect garden setting for afternoon tea.

7. Melinsey Mill
D5 Veryan, Roseland 01872 501049
Scones are served beside a peaceful pond in this 16th-century watermill.

8. Watersmeet House
A lovely spot for tea and cakes *(p99)*.

9. Hotel Meudon
Enjoy scones and tea in the verdant gardens of this coastal hotel *(p118)*, or splash out on a full afternoon tea.

10. Rectory Farm and Tea Rooms
E2 Crosstown, Morwenstow, near Bude Easter–Oct rectory-tearooms.co.uk
Feast on cakes and scones – there are gluten- and dairy-free options – beside an open fire in a 13th-century farm house.

CORNWALL AND DEVON FOR FREE

Mount Edgcumbe, one of Cornwall's finest country estates

1 Mount Edgcumbe

Although there is a fee to enter the house *(p84)*, access to the grounds – with more than 350 ha (865 acres) of beautiful parkland, formal gardens and the National Camellia Collection – is free. There are walks along the seashore among rare trees and plants, as well as a chance of glimpsing wild fallow deer.

2 Falmouth Art Gallery

The family-friendly Falmouth Art Gallery *(p49)* has a collection of 2,000 artworks, ranging from Pre-Raphaelite paintings to contemporary prints, photographs and children's illustrations. It also has the UK's largest public collection of automata. There are workshops for families and a changing programme of exhibitions.

3 Marconi Centre, Poldhu

B6 Near Mullion
Hours vary, check website
marconi-centre-poldhu.org.uk

This small heritage centre was built on the site from which Guglielmo Marconi transmitted the first ever transatlantic radio message to Signal Hill, St John's, Newfoundland on 12 December 1901. A short video presentation and information boards relate the fascinating story.

Ancient stone structures, Merrivale Prehistoric Settlement

4 Seaton Wetlands

M4 Colyford Rd, Seaton
wildeastdevon.co.uk

An excellent nature reserve, criss-crossed by boardwalks and trails that link bird hides and viewpoints overlooking a tidal saline lagoon. There's a small café and volunteer-run information centre, and the nostalgic Seaton Tramway *(tram.co.uk)* stops nearby.

5 Roskilly's Ice Cream Farm

C6 Tregellast Barton Farm, St Keverne roskillys.co.uk

Roskilly's Cornish ice cream is enjoyed across the county and beyond. At this organic farm you can watch the cows being milked as well as sample the ice cream. There are also marked trails through the meadows, and goats, pigs, sheep, turkeys, ducks and chickens can be seen along the way. The farm also has a restaurant and campsite.

6 Merrivale Prehistoric Settlement, Dartmoor

H4 On B3357, W of Princetown
english-heritage.org.uk

Merrivale is home to the remains of a Bronze Age village of round houses and several ritual structures, including three stone rows, a stone circle, standing stones and burial mounds. These monuments were built between 2500 and 1000 BCE, but one of the most distinctive stones is medieval – a huge round of granite once used for crushing cider apples.

7 Buckfast Abbey

The abbey *(p106)* and its grounds, including a lavender garden and a physic garden where medicinal herbs are cultivated, is home to Benedictine monks. There is also a shop selling crafts and produce made by monks and nuns from all over Europe.

8 Geocaching in Devon

Devon is a perfect location for geocaching *(geocaching.com)* – treasure-hunting via smartphone – with more than 25,000 geocaches scattered along its vast network of paths and cycle tracks. Geocachers use GPS to hide containers and then post clues to help others.

9 Shoalstone Pool, Brixham

K5 Berry Head Rd
May–Sep shoalstonepool.com

This Art Deco lido was built in 1926, with a seawater swimming pool dating from 1896, and is maintained by volunteers and the local council. There is a fee for parking and for those who decide to hire a beach hut or lounger.

10 Carn Euny Ancient Village

A5 Sancreed, Penzance
english-heritage.org.uk

The well-preserved Iron Age settlement of Carn Euny remained in use even during the Roman era. It features the remains of several round houses, a holy well and a fogou – an underground structure unique to western Cornwall – which visitors can walk through today.

TOP 10 BUDGET TIPS

1. Walks and Hikes
Cornwall and Devon have plenty of walking routes – not least a section of the South West Coast Path *(p59)*.

2. Pack a Picnic
Pop into a local supermarket or farm shop to stock up on lunch snacks – perfect for enjoying on the beach or part way along a hike.

3. Stay Inland
Accommodation inland and off the beaten track in Cornwall can be good value, while still within easy driving distance of the coast.

4. Wine and Cider Tastings
Free tastings are often held at vineyards and cider farms around the counties.

5. Bus Passes
In Devon, the Gold 7-Day MegaRider ticket gives access to all routes run by Stagecoach South West *(stagecoachbus.com)*.

6. Camp or Self-Cater
Staying on a campsite or in self-catering accommodation is often cheaper than a hotel.

7. Take the Sleeper
Save time – and a night's stay – by travelling on the Night Riviera train from London Paddington to Cornwall.

8. Cornwall Heritage Trust Membership
Membership gives free entry to all English Heritage sites in Cornwall.

9. Discount Vouchers
Look out for vouchers giving discounted entry to sights or special deals in cafés and restaurants. They can be found at most regional tourist offices.

10. Multiday Tickets
Entry tickets at many attractions in Cornwall and Devon are valid for seven days and some – including for the Eden Project *(p24)* and the National Marine Aquarium *(p48)* – are valid for a year.

FESTIVALS

1 Obby Oss, Padstow

1 May (or 2 May if date falls on Sun)
Pagan fertility rites and local traditions unite in this May Day spectacle. The main character, the Obby Oss *(p35)*, garbed in a black costume draped around a 2-m- (6-ft-) wide hoop, is accompanied by a "Teazer" with music, drumming and the May Song.

2 Helston's Flora Day

8 May (or previous Sat if date falls on Sun or Mon) W helstonflora day.org.uk
A uniquely Cornish extravaganza, Helston's Flora Day involves a stately procession of revellers in top hats or fancy frocks performing the "Furry Dance" through the streets of the town.

3 The du Maurier Fowey Literary Festival

Mid-May W foweyfestival.com
An eight-day literary celebration, this festival honours Daphne du Maurier – who once called Fowey home – while showcasing contemporary writers through music, drama, walks, workshops and daily talks.

4 Golowan Festival, Penzance

Late Jun W golowanfestival.org
This ten-day arts and dance festival features processions, circus acts, buskers and a mock mayoral election. Live music, flaming torches and fireworks are all part of the spectacle.

5 Cornwall Pride

Late Jul W cornwallpride.org
Cornwall's LGBTQ+ community celebrates Pride all summer long, with events like Newquay Pride in late July. Expect vibrant parades with floats, entertainment, crafts, walking bands and barbecues.

6 Sidmouth Folk Festival

Early Aug W sidmouthfolk festival.co.uk
Folk music, Northumbrian pipes and Morris dancers feature at a seaside festival in one of Devon's most elegant

One of the world's largest pride flags, Cornwall Pride

Street parade during the Golowan Festival, Penzance

towns. Even non-folk fans succumb to the event's upbeat charm, with buskers lining the Esplanade and pubs jammed with carousers. Accommodation and concert tickets sell out quickly.

7 St Ives September Festival

Mid-Sep W stivesseptember festival.co.uk

The arts have long been a strong presence in St Ives and this two-week jamboree brings them together with exhibitions, drama and poetry readings. Music ranges from cello recitals to tribute pop acts and African beats, with most performances held at the Guildhall and the Western Hotel. There are also talks and comedy shows.

8 Oyster Festival, Falmouth

Mid-Oct W falmouthoyster festival.co.uk

A four-day celebration of Cornish seafood, the Oyster Festival features music from local bands, oyster shucking competitions, cooking demonstrations and boat races.

9 Tar Barrelling, Ottery St Mary

5 Nov (or previous Sat if date falls on Sun) W tarbarrels.co.uk

Every Bonfire Night, tar-soaked barrels are set alight and hoisted around town and there are races for both adults and children. The evening culminates in fireworks and a huge bonfire beside the River Otter.

10 Tom Bawcock's Eve, Mousehole

23 Dec

A procession and fireworks display honour the fishers who once saved the village from starvation by going to sea in a storm and landing a huge catch of pilchards, which were served up in stargazy pie *(p67)*; you can sample the dish during the festivities.

TOP 10 LIVE MUSIC AND THEATRE VENUES

Open-air Minack Theatre

1. Minack Theatre
This amphitheatre *(p87)* hosts a range of productions in summer.

2. Theatre Royal, Plymouth
P5 Royal Parade
W theatreroyal.com
Popular shows are held in this large theatre in Plymouth.

3. Eden Project
This is Cornwall's best outdoor music venue *(p24)* in summer.

4. The Poly, Falmouth
C5 24 Church St W thepoly.org
Year-round venue for exhibitions, art cinema, theatre and concerts.

5. Hall for Cornwall, Truro
C5 Back Quay
W hallforcornwall.co.uk
Drama and music are staged here.

6. Exeter Northcott Theatre
N1 Stocker Rd
W exeternorthcott.co.uk
Exeter's principal theatrical venue.

7. Acorn Arts Centre, Penzance
B5 Parade St
W theacornpenzance.com
Once a church, this is now a playhouse.

8. Calstock Arts Centre, Calstock
F3 The Old Chapel
W calstockarts.org
Calstock's arts centre hosts a wide range of live music, theatre and comedy.

9. Barbican Theatre, Plymouth
Q6 Castle St
W barbicantheatre.co.uk
A theatre specializing in new drama.

10. Exeter Phoenix
This is Exeter's premier arts centre *(p49)*.

AREA BY AREA

The village of Clovelly, Devon

NORTH CORNWALL

With the Atlantic hammering on its coast, North Cornwall feels harsher than the county's more sheltered southern seaboard. Abandoned engine houses and chimney stacks recall its industrial past, while numerous Wesleyan chapels reveal the faith of its mining population. Between the cliffs are some of the region's best surf beaches. You can enjoy fine seafood in Padstow, explore historic buildings at Prideaux Place and Lanhydrock, and discover Arthurian connections, not least in the ruins at Tintagel.

1 Tintagel Castle

D2 Tintagel Hours vary, check website english-heritage.org.uk

This coastal stronghold is one of the country's most romantic castle ruins. Its appeal is enhanced by its Arthurian associations; it is the supposed birthplace of the Once and Future King. The structure, however, probably dates from the 12th century, when it belonged to

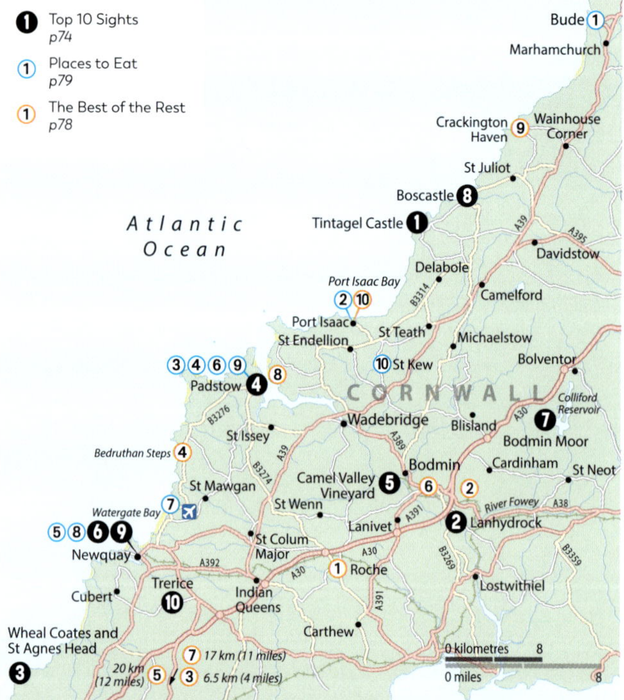

For places to stay in this area, see p116

Exploring the ruins of Tintagel Castle

the Norman earls of Cornwall. There may already have been a Roman fortification and traces of a Celtic monastery have been found here, too.

2 Lanhydrock

The finest house in Cornwall *(p22)* was originally Jacobean, but little of it survived a fire in 1881, which makes the Victorian interior visible today – restored by the National Trust – all the more astonishing. It comprises some 50 rooms, including the maids' quarters and the lavish rooms of the Agar-Robartes family, but the highlights are the impressive kitchens and sculleries. The gardens and parkland are worth exploring.

3 Wheal Coates and St Agnes Head

C4–C5 St Agnes Dusk–dawn daily nationaltrust.org.uk

Of all Cornwall's many former tin mines, those scattered along the St Agnes Heritage Coast might be the most dramatically sited. As you follow the rocky, coastal trail you'll come across the skeletons of several engine houses against the backdrop of the North Atlantic, plus the secluded cove of Chapel Porth.

4 Padstow

A picturesque fishing port set amid stunning beaches, Padstow *(p34)* is also Cornwall's gastronomic capital, synonymous with gourmet food since seafood champion Rick Stein established a restaurant here in the 1970s. This charming town is also part of the ancient pilgrim route known as the Saints' Way *(p58)*, and has a pretty working harbour that may have been in use as far back as 2500 BCE. The beaches nearby attract both surfers and families, and the sheltered Camel Estuary has great walking and cycling routes.

Boats docked at the harbour, Padstow

5 Camel Valley Vineyard

D4 Nanstallon, Bodmin 10am–5pm Mon–Fri camelvalley.com

Set on the slopes of the Camel Valley, this vineyard, founded in 1989, is the largest in Cornwall. It grows a number of grape varieties and produces a range of sparkling, red, white and rosé wines, many of which feature on the wine lists of the region's top restaurants. From April to September, guided tours are available daily at 10:30am. Visitors can also browse the on-site shop or enjoy a glass of wine on the picturesque terrace.

6 Newquay's Beaches

C4

Newquay developed as a beach resort after the railway arrived in the 1870s, and is now one of Britain's pre-eminent surf resorts, hosting numerous competitions at Fistral Beach. Holywell Bay and Perran Beach are also highly regarded surfing spots, while the more sheltered Towan Beach, Tolcarne and Lusty Glaze are better for families. Watergate Bay attracts the extreme sports crowd, but is just as good for a seaside walk.

7 Bodmin Moor

E3

Cornwall's great inland wilderness is made of the same granite mass as Dartmoor and has the same mixture of rugged grandeur interspersed with splashing rivers and shady woodland. Dotted with prehistoric remains such as the Hurlers and Trethevy Quoit, the moor has a plethora of places associated with King Arthur and his knights. It also has the distinction of being a World Heritage Site. The mining industry here is nearly 4,000 years old. In the midst of the desolate expanses lie appealing villages, such as Blisland, St Neot's and Altarnun.

8 Boscastle

D2

The great wall of cliffs comprising much of North Cornwall's coast is sliced through here by the Valency and Jordan rivers, which twist through a ravine to a harbour. Stroll through the

CORNWALL'S MINEWORKS

An iconic image of the Cornish landscape is the engine house and chimney that denote the existence of a former mine. North Cornwall is dotted with these castle-like granite structures, which hark back to a time when the county was producing up to two-thirds of the world's copper and tin. The industry fell into decline in the 1870s.

River Valency flowing down to the harbour at Boscastle

village before heading up to Warren Point or the Willapark Lookout for sweeping views of the coastline. Keep an eye out for the blowhole known as Devil's Bellows, below Penally Point.

9 Newquay Zoo

C4 Trenance Gardens newquayzoo.org.uk

This zoo holds more than 130 species and has an active conservation and education agenda. Visitors can meet the animals and watch them being fed. Look out for the graceful red pandas and comical lemurs, plus plenty of colourful birds and reptiles.

10 Trerice

C4 Kestle Mill, Newquay Hours vary, check website nationaltrust.org.uk

This National Trust-owned Elizabethan manor features an impressive barrel-roofed Great Chamber and a small yet beautifully designed formal garden. Outside in the grounds, you can try your hand at kayles – traditional Cornish skittles –or visit the hayloft for family-friendly activities like brass rubbing and dressing up in Tudor-style clothing.

Dramatic granite tor at Bodmin Moor

A DRIVE ALONG CORNWALL'S NORTHERN COAST

Morning

Cornwall's northernmost resort of **Bude** has fine beaches for a morning dip. From here, the A39 plunges south; branch off onto the B3263 to **Boscastle** for a stroll along its harbour and to explore the **Museum of Witchcraft and Magic** *(p49)*. Then, stop at **St Juliot's Church**, where Thomas Hardy once worked as an architect. Travel 6 km (4 miles) to **Tintagel** *(p74)* – its ruined castle is said to have been King Arthur's birthplace. After touring the ruins, grab lunch in a local café, or head south to the harbour village of **Port Isaac** *(p78)*.

Afternoon

After lunch, head inland to drive to Bodmin, an ancient market town. You can also visit **Bodmin Jail** *(p78)* for an immersive criminal history experience, or take a trip to nearby **Cardinham Woods** *(p78)* for a relaxing forest walk. From here, take the A30 west to **Newquay**, which has some of Cornwall's best beaches and a conservationist zoo. You can head up the coast on the B3276 and stop at **Watergate Bay** *(p56)*, where The Beach Hut *(p79)* is a great spot for snacks and surfing; hire equipment at Wavehunters *(wavehunters.co.uk)*. For dinner, continue up the B3276 to **Padstow** *(p34)*, which has a wide range of seafood restaurants.

The Best of the Rest

Stunning sea stacks, Bedruthan Steps

1. Roche Rock Hermitage

D4

Situated on top of a dramatic granite outcrop are the ruins of a chapel built as a hermitage in 1409. It is associated with numerous Cornish folk tales.

2. Cardinham Woods

E3 forestryengland.uk

There are four forest walks and three waymarked trails for mountain-bikers, plus a café and picnic areas.

3. Callestick Farm

C5 Callestick, Truro 10:30am–5pm daily callestickfarm.co.uk

Watch ice cream being made using clotted cream from the milk of the farm's cattle – and sample it, too.

4. Bedruthan Steps

C3

The jagged slate outcrops on this beach were said to be the stepping stones of the legendary giant, Bedruthan. At its western end, there's an excellent clifftop tearoom at Carnewas, offering stunning views.

5. East Pool Mine

B5 Pool, near Redruth Hours vary, check website nationaltrust.org

One of several former mines in the area, now owned by the National Trust, this site offers a fascinating glimpse into Cornwall's mining heritage. It houses two preserved engine houses and a discovery centre. Visitors can also watch an educational film to learn about the region's mining past.

6. Bodmin Jail

D4 Berrycoombe Rd, Bodmin Hours vary, check website bodminjail.org

Visits to this 1779 jail include tours of the "execution pit" and the cells, as well as the Dark Walk, an immersive experience of the jail's haunting past.

7. Porthtowan

C4

Home to several cafés and restaurants, this village features scenic clifftop walks and even a tidal pool. Its family-friendly beach is a favourite with surfers.

8. St Enodoc

D3 Daymer Bay 7:30am–dusk daily northcornwallcluster ofchurches.org.uk

The tiny 13th-century St Enodoc church appears hidden amid dunes on a golf course. Poet John Betjeman is buried here.

9. Crackington Haven

E2

This beach is backed by cliffs rising up to 130 m (430 ft), with rock strata at unusual angles.

10. Port Isaac

D3

A North Cornish fishing village, Port Isaac is known for its winding lanes and working harbour.

Places to Eat

1. Life's a Beach

E2 Summerleaze Cres, Bude
lifesabeach.info · ££

Overlooking the Atlantic, this café serves baguettes and burgers during the day. By night it is a classy candlelit bistro with a focus on seafood.

2. Outlaw's New Road

D3 6 New Rd, Port Isaac
01208 880896 Sun & Mon · £££

Chef and writer Nathan Outlaw's fish and seafood restaurant serves a single set tasting menu based around the morning's catch.

3. Stein's Fish & Chips

D3 South Quay, Padstow
rickstein.com · £

The most affordable and relaxed of Stein's restaurants, this place serves succulent fish and chips – battered or grilled – with gluten-free options also available.

4. The Seafood Restaurant

D3 Riverside, Padstow
rickstein.com · £££

The menu at Rick Stein's classy flagship restaurant features dishes familiar from the celebrity chef's books and TV programmes, along with newer creations.

5. Rick Stein Fistral

C4 Fistral Beach, Newquay
rickstein.com · £

Served in simple cardboard boxes, but enjoyed in a stunning setting, the food here ranges from classic fish and chips to tasty pad Thai and Goan chicken curry.

6. St Petroc's Bistro

D3 4 New St, Padstow
rickstein.com · ££

Smaller than the Seafood Restaurant, this Stein venture has fewer choices on the menu and lower prices, but still delivers the goods. Meat is given equal billing with seafood.

PRICE CATEGORIES

For a three-course meal for one with half a bottle of wine, including taxes and extra charges.

£ under £35 ££ £35–£55 £££ over £55

7. The Beach Hut

C4 Watergate Bay
01637 860543 · ££

With its gorgeous beachside location, this is a casual place for summer evenings. Fish specials and burgers are mainstays of the menu.

8. Lewinnick Lodge

C4 Pentire Headland, Newquay
lewinnicklodge.co.uk · ££

Seafood is the speciality at this coastal restaurant. Take in the views from the terrace or dine in the main restaurant.

9. Paul Ainsworth at No. 6

D3 6 Middle St, Padstow
01841 532093 Sun & Mon · £££

Dress up for dinner in this Georgian townhouse with contemporary decor and sophisticated food.

10. St Kew Inn

D3 St Kew, Bodmin
stkewinn.co.uk · ££

This 15th-century inn uses locally sourced seasonal produce in their dishes and offers cask ales.

The quaint setting of St Petroc's Bistro

SOUTH CORNWALL

With its undulating coastline, river estuaries interspersed with small settlements and historic towns, South Cornwall is ripe for exploration. Fowey and fishing villages such as Polperro should not be missed, while Cornwall's capital, Truro, is just small enough to negotiate on foot. The region's most famous attraction is the Eden Project, although South Cornwall's other major gardens, Trelissick and Heligan, are also essential stops. To the south, the Roseland Peninsula offers sandy coves and plenty of places to stay, eat and drink.

1 Fal Estuary

The largest of Cornwall's tidal river estuaries, the Fal *(p26)* is an ancient river valley, drowned at the end of the last ice age, when glaciers melted. From its source near St Austell, the Fal meets up with five other rivers and numerous small tidal creeks to flow into the estuary. It is 34 m (140 ft) at its deepest point. Along the river are more than 4,500 moorings for crafts, from yachts to deep water freighters, which often congregate here between contracts.

For places to stay in this area, see p117

Picturesque fishing village of Polperro

2 Polperro

E4

At peak times, this Cornish fishing village is overcrowded, but visit out of season, or early in the morning, and you can appreciate its charm. A long main street leads down to a huddle of houses, shops and restaurants around the harbour, making it perfect for evening walks, shopping and dining. Visitors can also wander the harbour, take a boat trip, browse local art at the Ebenezer Gallery *(ebenezergallery.co.uk)* or explore the smuggling and fishing museum housed in an old pilchard factory.

3 Eden Project

Since opening in a former clay pit in 2001, this site *(p24)* has been one of Cornwall's success stories. A "living theatre of plants and people", it is a great illustration of the diversity of the planet's plant life and makes for a perfect visit at any time of year. Thanks to its unique venue, the Eden Project is also a popular place to host musical performances, with world-renowned musicians performing in these "Eden Sessions". Over the years, it has welcomed artists such as Snow Patrol, Amy Winehouse, Elton John, Bastille and the Kaiser Chiefs.

4 Cornwall Museum & Art Gallery

C5 River St, Truro 10am–4pm daily cornwallmuseum.org

Home to a treasure trove of art and artifacts, the Cornwall Museum & Art Gallery (formerly the Royal Cornwall Museum) chronicles the rich history of the county. It's a cornucopia of Cornish culture, with everything from Bronze Age pottery to Newlyn art, plus mineral and fossil collections. Botanical and zoological specimens include stuffed puffins, butterflies and shells.

Pensilva
St Ann's Chapel
Callington
6 Cotehele House
A390
Bere Alston
St Mellion
Liskeard
A388
Bere Ferrers
Menheniot
Landulph
A38
A387
Deviock
Saltash
A374
St Germans
1 West Looe
Plymouth
9 Looe
Looe Bay
Whitesand Bay
4
Cowsand
Rame Head

1 Top 10 Sights p80
1 Places to Eat p85
1 The Best of the Rest p84

***The Mud Maid* by Susan Hill, Lost Gardens of Heligan**

5 Lost Gardens of Heligan

D4 Pentewan, St Austell
Hours vary, check website
heligan.com

"Lost" for 70 years and neglected for even longer, these salvaged Victorian gardens are a triumph of horticultural design. Home to a splendid pageantry of plants in a variety of habitats, including ferneries, fruit houses, Italian gardens and a kitchen garden, this subtropical "Jungle" and "Lost Valley" appeals to both adults and kids.

6 Cotehele House

H5 St Dominick, Saltash
Hours vary, check website
nationaltrust.org.uk

The excellent condition of this Tudor abode is due to its abandonment by its owners, the Edgcumbe family, who left it intact for a home outside Plymouth. The National Trust took it over in 1947. The house has many original pieces of furniture, suits of armour, and a collection of embroideries and tapestries that are best seen on a bright day as the rooms have no electric light.

7 Trelissick Garden

C5 King Harry, Feock
10am–5pm daily (Nov–mid-Feb: to 4:30pm) nationaltrust.org.uk

This lovely, extensive garden has lawns, flowerbeds as well as hollows filled with rare plants and shrubs, sprawling parkland as well as miles of woodland paths with panoramic views of the River Fal. Late April, early May and September are the best times to visit. The *King Harry* chain ferry, supposedly founded by King Henry VIII after spending his honeymoon with Anne Boleyn in St Mawes *(p84)*, crosses the River Fal below the garden, allowing direct access to the Roseland Peninsula – the round trip by road is 43 km (27 miles).

8 St Austell

D4

A busy industrial town, St Austell has been the heart of Cornwall's local china industry since it rose to prominence in

THE CHINA CLAY STORY

No one passing through the St Austell area can fail to notice the vast conical spoil heaps linked to the local china clay industry. The substance is used in a variety of products, from paint and paper to medicines. You can learn about its history and applications at the fascinating Wheal Martyn *(p84)*.

Boats in the charming harbour at Fowey

the 18th century. It's most famous for the Wheal Martyn China Clay Museum *(p84)*, which explores the history and human impact of clay mining. Other attractions include the sandy beaches of St Austell Bay.

9 Looe
E4

A fishing village and seaside resort, Looe straddles the mouth of its homonymous river, its two sides connected by a seven-arched bridge. A popular holiday spot since Victorian times, it continues to attract crowds today with its classic British seaside charm and its daily harbourside fish market, famous for its fresh local catches.

10 Fowey
E4

Climbing up the west bank of the River Fowey, this was one of the foremost ports of medieval England and is still a busy harbour town. Most of today's maritime activity, however, involves the pleasure boats anchored in the estuary. It is worth hiring a boat to fully enjoy the beauty of the river. A passenger ferry also connects Fowey to the quaint village of Polruan, which has access to the South West Coast Path.

A DRIVING TOUR IN SOUTH CORNWALL

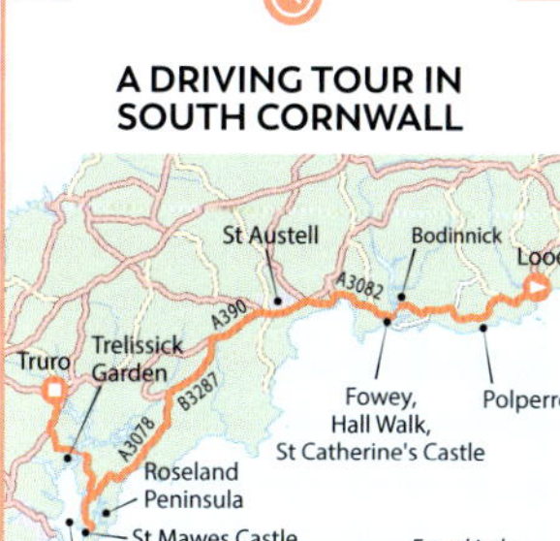

Morning

Start your journey in **Looe**, a traditional resort with an eponymous river that runs through the town. A 6-km (4-mile) drive from here takes you to **Polperro** *(p81)*, which is best appreciated before the crowds arrive. There is a small smuggling and fishing museum here. From Polperro, a scenic minor road leads you west to **Bodinnick** village, where ferries cross to **Fowey**. The port town has pubs and bistros that make for a good lunch stop. Before or after eating, take a stroll around Fowey to see **St Catherine's Castle**, one of Henry VIII's fortifications, or follow the 6-km (4-mile) **Hall Walk**, climbing through woodland above the harbour to Penleath Point for tremendous views.

Afternoon

From Fowey, take the A3082 to **St Austell**, from which the A390, B3287 and A3078 will bring you to St Mawes on the **Fal (Carrick Roads) Estuary**. Here, **St Mawes Castle** *(p84)* offers stunning views, while the wider **Roseland Peninsula** *(p59)* features quiet beaches and churches. Enjoy walks at **Trelissick Garden**, then take the *King Harry* chain ferry across the river. From here, it's a short drive to **Truro**, the county capital, known for its excellent restaurants and museum.

Elegant 19th-century Caerhays Castle

The Best of the Rest

1. Truro Cathedral

C5 St Mary's St, Truro 10am–5pm Mon–Sat, 11:30am–4:30pm Sun trurocathedral.org.uk

Truro's Gothic Revival cathedral has a soaring nave, with its tower and roof offering spectacular views. Visitors can also enjoy listening to the choir.

2. Restormel Castle

E4 Lostwithiel Apr–Sep: 10am–5pm daily; Oct: 10am–4pm daily english-heritage.org.uk

The parapet of this 13th-century keep has great views over the Fowey Valley.

3. Wheal Martyn China Clay Museum

D4 Wheal Martyn, St Austell 10am–5pm daily wheal-martyn.com

This mining museum provides a fascinating insight into the china-clay industry.

4. Mount Edgcumbe

F4 Cremyll, Torpoint Hours vary, check website mountedgcumbe.gov.uk

Rebuilt after World War II, this 16th-century house displays Chinese porcelain and Flemish tapestries.

5. Castle Dore

E4 Golant

This Iron Age hillfort, with its concentric rings of defensive ridges, is considered to be the site of the palace of the legendary figure, King Mark of Cornwall.

6. Caerhays Castle

D5 Gorran, St Austell Hours vary, check website visitcaerhays.co.uk

Explore the beautifully landscaped gardens at this 19th-century castle, located near St Austell.

7. St Mawes Castle

C5 St Mawes Apr–Oct: 10am–5pm daily english-heritage.org.uk

One of two 16th-century artillery forts near the Fal Estuary, this castle is better preserved than Pendennis and features heraldic symbols dedicated to Henry VIII and Edward VI.

8. Mevagissey

D5

With its long tradition of fishing and smuggling, this busy port is worth visiting for its museum and restaurants.

9. Veryan

D5

Close to good beaches, Veryan is known for its 200-year-old circular houses designed to prevent the devil from hiding in corners.

10. St Just-in-Roseland

C5 St Just-in-Roseland 8:30am–4pm daily stjustandstmawes.org.uk

UK Poet Laureate John Betjeman once described this church as "to many people the most beautiful churchyard on Earth". Nestled beside a tidal creek, it has a peaceful garden.

Places to Eat

1. The Sardine Factory

G5 West Looe thesardinefactorylooe.com Mon & Tue · ££

Tuck into dishes like Cornish hake served with *roti* (flatbread) and curry-fried onions at this seafood restaurant.

2. Castle Beach Café

C5 Cliff Rd, Falmouth 01326 617210 · £

Plenty of vegan and gluten-free options are on the menu at this beachside café.

3. St Mawes Hotel

C5 Harbourside, St Mawes stmaweshotel.com · ££

A relaxed brasserie serving simple dishes at lunch and dinner, such as lobster and chips and homemade pizza.

4. Beach House Falmouth

C5 Swanpool Beach, Falmouth beachhousefalmouth.com · £££

This beachside terrace restaurant serves fresh local seafood, including Falmouth Bay lobsters and tasty cocktails.

5. The Hidden Hut

C5 Porthcurnick Beach, Portscatho, Truro hiddenhut.co.uk · £

A beach café in a hut perched above sandy Porthcurnick cove, serving lunches, soups, coffees and cakes.

6. Gylly Beach Café

C5 Cliff Rd, Falmouth gyllybeach.com · ££

This Falmouth institution is perfect for breakfast, lunch, cakes or dinner, with splendid views over Gyllyngvase Beach.

7. Muddy Beach

C5 Commercial Rd, Penryn muddybeach.com · ££

Muddy Beach is the ideal spot to enjoy a hearty brunch or lunch, or evening small plates, cocktails and live music.

PRICE CATEGORIES

For a three-course meal for one with half a bottle of wine, including taxes and extra charges.

£ under £35 **££** £35–£55 **£££** over £55

8. Hotel Tresanton

C5 27 Lower Castle Rd, St Mawes thepolizzicollection.com/hotel-tresanton · £££

Modern Mediterranean food is served in this chic seaside hotel. A terrace offers scenic alfresco dining.

9. The Old Quay House

E4 Old Quay House, 28 Fore St, Fowey theoldquayhouse.com · £££

Set within the Old Quay House hotel, this riverside restaurant pairs splendid views over the River Fowey with equally fabulous food.

10. Edie's

D4 10 Beach Rd, Carlyon Bay edies.restaurant · ££

Expect exquisitely prepared food at this family-run restaurant, which focuses on locally sourced ingredients. The prix-fixe menu is great value.

Façade of the St Mawes Hotel

WEST CORNWALL AND THE ISLES OF SCILLY

For many, the western tip of Cornwall embodies what makes the county so special. Here, you can find every kind of landscape Cornwall has to offer, from the rugged moorland of the Penwith Peninsula and the wild cliffs at Zennor to the sandy swathes of Whitesand Bay and the turquoise coves of Lizard Point. This scenic region is also home to a number of key Cornish towns, including the university hub of Falmouth and artist haven of St Ives. But if you're looking to escape it all, the isolated Isles of Scilly await.

For places to stay in this area, see p117

Cornwall's most iconic landmark, St Michael's Mount

1 Penzance

Penzance *(p32)* possesses two of Cornwall's best museum-galleries – Penlee House and the Exchange *(p49)* – and plenty of historical character in the handsome buildings of Chapel Street. From the town, all the glories of the Penwith Peninsula are easily accessible, from St Michael's Mount to the coast's rocky coves and beaches.

2 St Michael's Mount

This castle residence in Mount's Bay *(p32)* can be reached by causeway or passenger ferry, followed by a steep climb up to the house itself. Inside, the most impressive rooms are the Tudor Great Hall and the dainty Blue Drawing Room. Other rooms hold armour, weaponry and memorabilia.

3 St Ives

The Mediterranean flavour of this seaside town *(p30)* is clearly visible with its maze of flowery lanes climbing up the hill. Its clear light and rugged landscape were a major draw for artists who settled here, renting studios from local fishers. Today, tourists have replaced pilchards as the town's mainstay, thronging its galleries, beaches and restaurants every summer. To escape the crowds, climb up to the island, which has views across St Ives Bay.

4 Minack Theatre

A6 Porthcurno, Penzance
Hours vary, check website
minack.com

The vision of one woman, Rowena Cade *(p29)*, the Minack is a unique attraction in Cornwall. Just like a Roman amphitheatre on some Mediterranean shore, the theatre has been carved out of the cliff face above the sea, creating a magical setting for plays and musicals. Shows are performed from April through to September.

Pretty hydrangeas in Trebah Garden

5 Trebah Garden

C5 Mawnan Smith
9:30am–5pm daily trebahgarden.co.uk

Subtropical Trebah is one of the most beautiful gardens in Cornwall, spilling down to the waters of the River Helford. Now owned by the Trebah Garden Trust, the gardens were created by Charles Fox, a Quaker, scientist and owner of an iron foundry, who paid meticulous attention to every detail.

6 Isles of Scilly

It takes some effort to reach the Isles of Scilly *(p42)*, but few come away disappointed. Imagined by some to be the remains of the legendary lost land of Lyonnesse, which sank below the waves after the last battle between Arthur and Mordred, this scattered archipelago is breathtakingly beautiful, sprinkled with tiny, jagged rocks and islets. Of the five inhabited islands, the main one is St Mary's. The chicest retreat is privately owned Tresco, home to the Abbey Gardens, while Bryher, St Martin's and St Agnes appeal to those who want to escape from contemporary life.

Dramatic rocky coastline of Land's End

7 Helford and Frenchman's Creek

C5

Known for its old-world charm, the riverside village of Helford has a fascinating history as a smugglers' haunt. Today, it's best known as the starting point for a scenic walk through oak woodlands to Frenchman's Creek – a spot that inspired one of Daphne du Maurier's novels.

8 Lizard Peninsula

C6–B6

As the southernmost peninsula in Britain, the Lizard is an area of extreme contrasts, stretching from the glassy waters, whitewashed villages and ancient oak woodland of the River Helford, across open heathland to serpentine cliffs, sculpted bays and fishing villages such as Cadgwith Cove. On the southwest edge of bleak Goonhilly Downs is stunning Kynance Cove *(p57)*.

9 Mousehole

A5

With its steep, cobbled alleyways and higgledy-piggledy houses, popular Mousehole is the quintessential Cornish fishing village. Its charm is at its peak just out of season, when you can enjoy its tiny harbour and views of St Michael's Mount without the crowds, or during Christmas, when the village is

STARGAZY PIE

According to legend, after a winter of storms when boats had been unable to put out to sea, Mousehole's residents were starving. On 23 December, fisher Tom Bawcock braved the storm and landed a huge catch of pilchards, which were then cooked up by the villagers into stargazy pie.

beautifully lit up. Half a mile inland at St Pol de Léon's Church in the village of Paul, is a monument to Dolly Pentreath, who died in 1777 and was said to be the last fluent native speaker of Cornish.

10 Land's End

A6

The westernmost tip of the British mainland holds a perennial fascination. The headland offers panoramic views over the coast and to rocky outcrops out at sea with intriguing names such as Dr Syntax Head and the Armed Knight. The Longships lighthouse, 2 km (1 mile) out, is also usually visible. At times you can spot Wolf Rock lighthouse, 15 km (9 miles) to the southwest, and even the Isles of Scilly, 45 km (28 miles) away.

A WALK FROM NEWLYN TO PORTHCURNO

Morning

If you're in **Newlyn** *(p90)* early enough, look in on the fish auction that takes place here every morning. Then, start your walk along a cycle-path running south from the harbour. After walking about 2 km (1 mile), you will reach the bijou fishing village of **Mousehole**, which was ransacked by a Spanish raiding party in 1595; they left just one building standing – **Keigwin Manor**. Walk through the village and pick up the coast path to reach **Point Spaniard** where the raiders supposedly landed. Further down the path is Carn Du, the eastern point of Lamorna Cove. Stop for lunch at the **Lamorna Cove Café** *(lamornacove.com/cafe)*.

Afternoon

From Lamorna the path sticks close to the rocky coast. Follow it to **St Loy's Cove**. For this stretch of the walk there are no cafés, so make sure you've stocked up with snacks. After a short walk, mainly on the clifftop, you will reach **Penberth Cove** – little more than a few cottages and fishing boats. Continue along the clifftop, past the Iron Age fort of **Treryn Dinas** *(p28)*, where you can see the famous **Logan Rock** *(p28)*. For dinner, follow the path down to **Porthcurno** *(p28)*, which has a café and pub, plus the **Minack Theatre** *(p87)*.

The Best of the Rest

Intricately designed maze at Glendurgan

1. Cornish Seal Sanctuary

B5 Gweek, Helston
10am–5pm daily sealsanctuary.sealifetrust.org

Sick or injured seals are brought here from all over the country. You can tour the pools and the hospital.

2. Gunwalloe

B6 nationaltrust.org.uk

There are many scenic coves along the western coast of the Lizard Peninsula, with several clustered near the village of Mullion. Among them, Gunwalloe is especially lovely, bordered by dunes and overlooked by a medieval church.

3. Helston

B5

Once a major river port and stannary town, Helston is home to the Museum of Cornish Life *(p49)*.

4. Tremenheere Sculpture Gardens

B5 Gulval, Penzance
Hours vary, check website
tremenheere.co.uk

Contemporary sculpture and art installations blend with lush subtropical planting in a sheltered valley.

5. Helford Passage

C5

This pretty village lies across the river from Helford. The Ferry Boat Inn *(p92)* terrace is a great place to watch the local gig rowers *(p43)* training.

6. The Tin Coast

A5 tincoast.co.uk

Wild West Penwith is home to some of Cornwall's most spectacular mining sites. From Geevor *(p62)*, the UK's largest preserved mine, you can walk to the jagged coastline and take in the breathtaking view of Botallack (or the Crowns) clinging to the clifftop at Cape Cornwall.

7. Newlyn

A5

One of Britain's most important fishing ports, Newlyn was home to an influential art movement in the late 19th and early 20th centuries. Works of Henry Scott Tuke and Stanhope Forbes are featured in the Newlyn Art Gallery.

8. Glendurgan

C5 Mawnan Smith Mid-Feb–Oct: 10:30am–5pm Tue–Sun (Aug: daily) nationaltrust.org.uk

Highlights of this lovely 19th-century wooded garden include azalea and camellia gardens and a popular cherry laurel hedge maze.

9. Western Rocks, Isles of Scilly

A4

These remote islands are breeding grounds for grey seals and several seabird species. Landing is prohibited, but there are boat trips to see shipwrecks and spot birds and seals.

10. Sennen Cove

A5

At the southern end of Whitesand Bay is the pretty village of Sennen Cove. Popular with surfers tackling the Atlantic rollers, its beach is patrolled by lifeguards throughout the summer.

Prehistoric Sites

1. Chun Castle

A5 Near Morvah, off B3318

The walls of this Iron Age hillfort are mainly collapsed, but in parts they reach a height of 3 m (9 ft), and the gateposts still stand.

2. Lanyon Quoit

A5 Near Morvah

Also known as the Giant's Quoit or Giant's Table, this capped burial chamber is one of the most accessible of West Penwith's prehistoric remains.

3. Halliggye Fogou

C6 Trelowarren, Mawgan, Helston english-heritage.org.uk

This is one of the most impressive of West Cornwall's fogous – long underground structures from the Iron Age.

4. Mên-an-Tol

A5 Near Morvah, off Morvah–Madron Rd

The Cornish name (which means stone-with-a-hole) accurately describes this Bronze Age monument that was long thought to have healing powers.

5. Chun Quoit

A5 Near Morvah, off B3318

On open moorland, this quoit – a neolithic chamber tomb topped by a flat stone and resembling a granite mushroom – dates from around 2000 BCE.

Ring-shaped stone at Mên-an-Tol

6. Tregiffian Burial Chamber

A6 Near Lamorna, off B3315 english-heritage.org.uk

This barrow tomb revealed a funerary urn and cremated bones when it was excavated in 1967.

7. The Merry Maidens

A6 Near Lamorna, off B3315

Considered Cornwall's most perfect stone circle, this is believed to be the remains of 19 maidens turned to stone for carousing on the Sabbath.

8. Chysauster

A5 Near Zennor Hours vary, check website english-heritage.org.uk

Cornwall's most complete prehistoric monument consists of stone-walled houses arranged around courtyards, where you can discern a number of hearths, basins and drains.

9. Bant's Carn, Isles of Scilly

B4 Halangy Down, St Mary's english-heritage.org.uk

This atmospheric burial chamber on St Mary's has a roof comprising four huge slabs.

10. Porth Hellick Down Burial Chamber, Isles of Scilly

B4 Porth Hellick Down, St Mary's english-heritage.org.uk

Located in the southeastern corner of St Mary's island, this is the best-preserved prehistoric tomb on the Isles of Scilly.

Cafés and Pubs

1. The Tinners Arms
A5 Zennor tinnersarms.com
The Tinners Arms has served the locals for more than 700 years. Enjoy a local Newlyn crab sandwich for lunch.

2. Pedn Olva
B5 West Portminster Beach, St Ives pednolva.co.uk
Owned by the St Austell Brewery, this pub is set on the promontory between St Ives' two beaches. The local goat's cheese with a beer is a must-try.

3. The Sloop Inn
B5 St Ives sloop-inn.co.uk
Savour a seafood platter and round off your meal with homemade gin, Cornish ales and lagers at this iconic pub.

4. New Inn
A4 Tresco, Isles of Scilly tresco.co.uk/eating/new-inn
A stylish pub offering excellent pub food, such as Bryher lobster and chips or Tresco beef burgers.

5. Blue Anchor Inn
B5 50 Coinagehall St, Helston spingoales.com/the-blue-anchor
Enjoy the medieval atmosphere at this former monks' resthouse. Cosy nooks and home-brewed Spingo ales are the main attractions.

6. Kynance Cove Beach Café
B5 Kynance Cove, Helston kynancecovecafe.co.uk
This beach café is housed in a former fisher's cottage. Its decked terrace is a perfect place to relax and watch the dramatic cove change with the rise and fall of the tide.

7. The Turks Head
A4 St Agnes, Isles of Scilly turksheadscilly.co.uk
Promising sea views and a welcoming community atmosphere, this pub serves Turks Ale, crab rolls and delicious Cornish pasties.

8. Ferry Boat Inn
C5 Helford Passage ferryboatcornwall.co.uk
With a terrace overlooking the River Helford, this inn is a popular pitstop for walkers on the coastal path.

9. The Crab Shack
A4 Bryher, Isles of Scilly 01722 422947 Oct–Apr
Sample mussels, scallops or crabs, with chips, salad and wine at this rustic restaurant.

10. Ship Inn
A5 South Cliff, Mousehole shipinnmousehole.co.uk
This fishers' pub above the harbour is full of maritime character. Battered catch of the day is usually on the menu.

Admiring the view from Kynance Cove

Restaurants

PRICE CATEGORIES

For a three-course meal for one with half a bottle of wine, including taxes and extra charges.

£ under £35 ££ £35–£55 £££ over £55

1. Kota Restaurant

B5 Harbour Head, Porthleven Sun & Mon kotarestaurant.co.uk · ££

Chef Jude adds an Asian twist to food made using organic Cornish produce at this harbourside restaurant.

2. Blas Burgerworks

B5 The Warren, St Ives blasburgerworks.co.uk · £

This lively gourmet burger restaurant in St Ives serves some excellent chargrilled Cornish burgers. Vegan options include a hearty black bean and kimchi-tofu burgers.

3. The Ruin Beach Café

B4 Tresco, Isles of Scilly 01720 424849 · ££

Beautifully styled restaurant housed in a former smugglers' cottage, with terrace seating and a contemporary Mediterranean menu, including pizzas from a wood-burning oven.

4. Porthminster Beach Café

B5 Porthminster Beach, St Ives 01736 795352 Mon in winter · ££

A beach café by day and a smart restaurant at night, this place serves dishes such as monkfish curry or crispy squid with miso dressing.

5. The First & Last Inn

A5 Sennen firstandlastinn.co.uk · ££

Just a mile from Land's End, this pub has been welcoming crowds since the 17th century. It now offers hearty meals and local ales beside an open fire or outside in the sheltered garden.

Distinctive yellow exterior of Gurnard's Head

6. Gurnard's Head

A5 Zennor gurnardshead.co.uk · £££

A stylish, relaxed gastro-pub serving Mediterranean dishes using fresh fish and locally sourced meat and produce.

7. Porthmeor Beach Café

B5 Porthmeor, St Ives porthmeor-beach.co.uk · ££

Located just above Porthmeor Beach *(p31)*, the food here is inspired by far-flung cuisines and the dessert tapas are sublime.

8. 2 Fore Street

A5 2 Fore St, Mousehole 2forestreet.co.uk · ££

Head to this relaxed French-style bistro right by the harbour for unfussy dishes such as Newlyn crab soufflé.

9. Juliet's Garden

B4 St Mary's, Isles of Scilly 01720 422228 Nov–Mar · ££

Enjoy a daytime snack or lunch with a view at this spot above Porthloo Beach.

10. Adam's Fish and Chips

B4 Higher Town, St Martin's, Isles of Scilly 01720 638506 Oct–Mar · £

Booking is essential at this family-run restaurant. Choose your own fish in advance.

NORTH DEVON

Between Exmoor and the rocky pinnacles of Hartland Point, North Devon crams in a rich landscape. Two of the region's top nature reserves, Northam Burrows and Braunton Burrows, and some of the best beaches, such as Woolacombe Bay, Saunton Sands and Westward Ho!, are located on this stretch of coast. Friendly towns such as Barnstaple and Ilfracombe and scenic coastal villages like Appledore and Clovelly are also worth visiting.

Puffins on a cliff on Lundy Island

1 Lundy Island

G1 landmarktrust.org.uk/lundyisland

This remote 5-km- (3-mile-) long sliver of land is located north of Hartland Point and is named after the puffins that live here ("lunde" is medieval Norse for puffin). There are options for overnight stays, including a lighthouse and a radio room. Day trips sail from Ilfracombe and Bideford in summer.

1 Top 10 Sights p94
1 Places to Eat p99
1 Beauty Spots p98

Lundy Island 1
North East Point
Tibbet's Point
Dead Cow Point
10 Lundy Island
Landing Bay
6
MARISCO CASTLE
Surf Point
0 km 1
0 miles 1

Atlantic Ocean
Lundy Island
Barnstaple or Bideford Bay
Hillsborough 4
Combe Martin
Ilfracombe 9
Mortehoe
Woolacombe
Woolacombe Bay 3
1
Arlington
Croyde
9 Tarka Trail
Croyde Bay
Muddiford
Shirwell
Saunton
Braunton
Saunton Sands 5
Ashford
4 Braunton Burrows 3
2 10
Barnstaple
Northam Burrows 7
2
5 Appledore
Bishop's Tawton
Westward Ho!
5
Abbotsham
6 Bideford
River Taw
3 Hartland Point
2 4
7 Clovelly
Alverdiscott
Stoke
Hartland
Dyke
Atherington
Weare Giffard 8
River Torridge
Woolfardisworthy
B3343
A3123
A399
A361
B3230
A39
B3231
A377

For places to stay in this area, see p118

2 Museum of Barnstaple and North Devon

H2 The Square, Barnstaple
10am–4:30pm Mon–Sat
barnstaplemuseum.org.uk

Home to exhibits on local wildlife and a gallery devoted to *Tarka the Otter (p96)*, this museum chronicles the rich history of this area. You can walk through a model Wellington bomber and view timepieces and glassware. The Barum Ware – fine pottery for which this area is renowned – is superb.

3 Woolacombe Bay

H1

Surfers know this impressive arc of sand as one of England's top sites for riding the waves, but non-surfers will find plenty of space here, especially at the more sheltered southern end, Putsborough. Rent gear or sign up for lessons at the shops and stalls above the beach. There are also a handful of cafés and bars here.

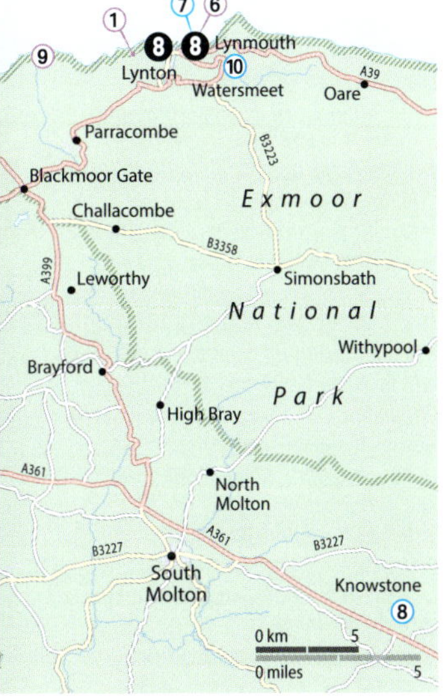

Braunton Burrows' extensive wild dune reserve

4 Braunton Burrows

H2

The core of a UNESCO-designated biosphere, this area constitutes the largest sand-dune system in the UK. It's locally known as the Burrows and gets its name from the hundreds of rabbit warrens dug into the dunes, although rabbit numbers have dropped significantly in recent years. The dunes are stabilized by marram grass and other plants; nearly 500 species of vascular plants and a variety of invertebrates live here. Meandering paths traverse the area, which can be reached on the Tarka Trail *(p58)* and the South West Coast Path *(p59)*.

5 Appledore

H2

A stately air hangs over this village of Georgian houses at the edge of the Torridge Estuary. Behind the seafront, narrow lanes with shops and pubs lead uphill to the Maritime Museum *(northdevonmaritimemuseum.co.uk)* with its collection of nautical items. For the best estuary views, tasty seafood and a pint, head for one of the two pubs on Irsha Street.

6 The Burton at Bideford

H2 Kingsley Rd, Bideford 10am–5pm Mon–Sat, 11am–4pm Sun burtonartgallery.co.uk

The "little white town" of Bideford – rich with historical associations and home of the Elizabethan mariner Sir Richard Grenville – houses the Burton Art Gallery and Museum. The gallery has an absorbing collection of art and artifacts, including watercolours, model ships and replicas of the famed local slipware. The museum is located in Victoria Park, where cannons taken from the Spanish Armada are exhibited.

7 Clovelly

G2 Hours vary, check website clovelly.co.uk

This picturesque settlement clings to a steep cliff and plunges down to a small harbour. The town is privately owned and cars are not allowed in, except for a Land Rover service for visitors who find the steep main street unmanageable. Some of the cottages are open to the public, including a museum dedicated to Charles Kingsley, author of *The Water Babies*, who lived here as a child.

8 Lynton and Lynmouth

J1

These villages on the Exmoor coast, linked by a water-powered funicular, have drawn visitors since the 1800s when the poet Percy Bysshe Shelley spent his honeymoon with his first wife here. Nestled among hills, the villages are a haven of tranquillity, though it was not always peaceful here. Lynmouth, by the sea, was devastated by a flash flood in 1952; the Glen Lyn Gorge, through which the torrent raged, holds an exhibition in memory of the event.

TARKA THE OTTER

The Tarka Line, Tarka Trail and Tarka Country all refer to *Tarka the Otter*, written by Henry Williamson. The book narrates the adventures of a young otter amid the beautiful landscape of North Devon – "the country of the two rivers". The book remains a classic animal tale, and was made into a film in 1979, narrated by Peter Ustinov.

Picturesque fishing village of Lynton

9 Tarka Trail

H1–H3

Henry Williamson's classic animal fable *Tarka the Otter* was set around his native North Devon. The otter's epic journeys are traced in this 290-km (180-mile) trail, which describes a figure of eight centred on the town of Barnstaple and incorporating sections of the South West Coast Path and Tarka Line railway. Over 50 km (31 miles) of the trail, between Braunton and Meeth, can be cycled. Other sections take in the scenic Taw Valley and Williamson's home village of Georgeham.

10 Barnstaple Pannier Market

H2 Butchers Row, Barnstaple 9am–4pm Tue–Sat northdevon.gov.uk/business

This covered market in the town centre is the most famous of Devon's

Places to Eat

Seafood shack at the Glorious Oyster, Instow

1. The Coach House

H2 Kentisbury Grange, Barnstaple 01271 545008 · £££

A stylish country hotel on the edge of Exmoor hosts this restaurant by Devon-born chef Michael Caines.

2. The Glorious Oyster

H2 Sandhills, Instow
01271 861209 Mon & Tue · £

Located in Instow, this cool little beach shack serves the day's freshest catch, be it oysters, mussels or prawns.

3. Fremington Quay Café

H2 Fremington Quay, Barnstaple 01271 268720 · £

This café is a perfect stop on the Tarka Trail from Barnstaple to Bideford, serving cakes, cream teas and lunch.

4. Red Lion

G2 48 The Quay, Clovelly
redlion-clovelly.co.uk · ££

This harbourside inn has great views and a menu that features locally caught fish and game from the Clovelly Estate.

5. M' Rock N' Bowl

H2 1 Ennisfarne Rd, Westward Ho!, Bideford 07745 085147 · ££

A friendly restaurant with stunning sea views, M' Rock N' Bowl focuses on traditional Moroccan cuisine.

PRICE CATEGORIES

For a three-course meal for one with half a bottle of wine, including taxes and extra charges.

£ under £35 **££** £35–£55 **£££** over £55

6. Marisco Tavern

G1 Lundy Island
01237 431831 · £

Lundy's sole pub serves island specialities using Soay lamb and venison from Sika deer. Highland cattle can be found near the tavern.

7. Rising Sun

J1 Harbourside, Lynmouth
risingsunlynmouth.co.uk · ££

Contemporary cuisine – featuring seafood – is served in a 14th-century inn that claims to have once accommodated poet Percy Bysshe Shelley.

8. The Masons Arms

J2 Knowstone, South Molton
01398 341231 Sun–Tue · £££

Set in a thatched 13th-century pub on the edge of Exmoor, this welcoming Michelin-starred restaurant offers excellent food and alfresco dining in good weather.

9. Lynbay Fish & Chip Shop

H1 6 The Quay, Ilfracombe
lynbayfish-chips.co.uk · £

A classic fish and chips meal awaits you at this take away spot right on the harbour. A menu for kids as well as gluten-free options are available.

10. Watersmeet House

J1 Watersmeet Rd, Lynmouth
01598 753348 Nov–mid-Mar: Mon–Fri · £

This Victorian fishing lodge is run by the National Trust and hosts an inviting tearoom and garden. There's plenty of outdoor seating.

SOUTH DEVON

A genteel atmosphere pervades much of South Devon. Verdant meadows are interspersed with cob-and-thatch villages, and rivers drift serenely through wooded valleys dotted with tidy cottages. Crumbling red cliffs rear above beaches, while in the forbidding expanse of Dartmoor, lonely tors punctuate slopes of bracken and gorse, and isolated communities are huddled around centuries-old churches. A world away from these rural scenes are the cathedral cities of Exeter and Plymouth, the region's historic power centres, both repositories of Devon's layered history, where medieval alleys, Elizabethan houses and Georgian terraces speak of a region shaped by conquest, trade and the sea.

For places to stay in this area, see p119

River Exe meandering through Exeter

1 Exeter

Devon's capital *(p38)* is a relaxed city with a historic core that includes the region's oldest cathedral and a museum. There's also a network of underground passages and an old quayside. The city has an active cultural life, with year-round festivals and events, and a good selection of restaurants.

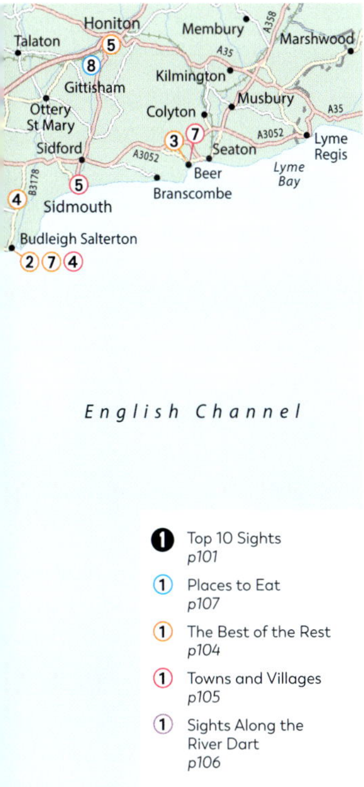

1 Top 10 Sights p101
1 Places to Eat p107
1 The Best of the Rest p104
1 Towns and Villages p105
1 Sights Along the River Dart p106

2 Dartmoor

In a region dominated by the sea, Dartmoor *(p36)* is a moorland where semi-wild ponies roam. Prehistoric remains are scattered across it, while on its edges lie the market towns of Okehampton and Tavistock. It also offers plenty of opportunities for walking, canoeing and wildlife watching.

3 A La Ronde

L4 Summer Lane, Exmouth
Hours vary, check website
nationaltrust.org.uk

When cousins Jane and Mary Parminter returned from their European travels in 1790, they brought with them trunkloads of souvenirs and a vision. They built this 16-sided house and filled it with mementos and quirky creations. These range from seaweed and sand concoctions to a shell-covered gallery.

Unique seashell fireplace, A La Ronde

4 Lydford Gorge

H4 The Stables, Lydford Apr–Sep: 10am–4:30pm daily; Oct: 10am–3:30pm daily nationaltrust.org.uk

On the edge of Dartmoor, the River Lyd gushes noisily through this oak-wooded ravine, home to the spectacular Devil's Cauldron whirlpool and the White Lady Waterfall that plummets 28 m (90 ft). There are walks along the river and a winding upper path but sturdy boots are required, and children must be supervised. Access to this point may be difficult for those with impaired mobility.

5 Torre Abbey

K5 King's Drive, Torquay 10am–5pm Tue–Sun torre-abbey.org.uk

One of Devon's best museums is housed in a mansion converted from abbey buildings after the Dissolution of the Monasteries in 1539. Its excellent 19th-century art collection includes works by William Holman Hunt and Edward Burne-Jones. The grounds hold medieval ruins and a tithe barn.

6 Powderham Castle

K4 Kenton Apr–Oct: 10am–4pm Sun–Fri powderham.co.uk

Surrounded by a deer park, this stately pile is the long-time seat of the earls of Devon. Tours take in the ornate music room, the majestic dining room, lavish bedrooms and the Victorian kitchen. There are kids' activity trails in the grounds.

7 Buckland Abbey

H5 Yelverton Mid-Feb–Oct: 11am–4:30pm daily nationaltrust.org.uk

The former home of Elizabethan mariners Richard Grenville and Francis Drake, this handsome manor house occupies beautiful grounds in the Tavy Valley. Visitors can look round the monastic Great Barn, Elizabethan Garden and the main Abbey, where galleries feature interactive displays. Exhibits include Drake's Drum, which, according to legend, will sound again when England is in danger to summon Drake from his grave.

DEVON'S RESORTS

Devon's south coast benefited from the 19th-century development and extension of Britain's railway network. With the influx of visitors, villas and *cottages ornés* (thatched, rustic dwellings) sprang up in fashionable towns such as Torquay, Exmouth and Sidmouth.

Distinctive Smeaton's Tower in Plymouth

8 Plymouth

H5

This historic city contains remnants of its Elizabethan glory days, notably in the harbourside Barbican quarter. Other attractions include the National Marine Aquarium *(p48)* and the Plymouth Gin Distillery *(p104)*. Don't miss the sea views from Plymouth Hoe, a high, grassy esplanade above the harbour.

9 Crediton Parish Church

K3 Church Ln, Crediton
creditonparishchurch.org.uk

Dating back to the 15th century, this red sandstone structure is one of Devon's grandest churches. Its east window features the key points in the life of the missionary St Boniface, who was born in 680 CE. The extensive and intricate memorial of 1911, occupying the east wall of the nave, is dedicated to Sir Redvers Buller. He was awarded the Victoria Cross in the 1879 Zulu War.

10 Crealy Theme Park & Resort

L4 Sidmouth Rd, Exeter Hours vary, check website crealy.co.uk

Devon's largest theme park, Crealy offers a fun-filled day out, with thrilling rides such as the Maximus Rollercoaster, the Tidal Wave Log Flume and the Crealy Grand Prix electric race track.

State Dining Room at Powderham Castle

A DRIVING TOUR IN SOUTH DEVON

Morning

Start close to the Dorset border at **Beer** *(p105)*, a village associated with the exploits of the smuggler Jack Rattenbury. You can grab a crab sandwich on the beach here. Follow the A3052 west to **Sidmouth** *(p105)*, whose seafront and esplanade are perfect for a stroll. The town is studded with villas from the Regency period. The museum here includes a lovely display of lace. Indulge in a hearty seaside lunch before leaving town.

Afternoon

Continuing west, just outside **Exmouth** *(p105)*, stop to admire **A La Ronde** *(p101)*, a 16-sided folly constructed by Jane and Mary Parminter. Go north to the M5, then take the A380 and A381 south to **Totnes** *(p105)*. Despite its free-spirited vibe, the town retains much of its Elizabethan character and also has a Norman castle and a 14th-century church. From Totnes, drive or take a river cruise along the **River Dart** to the sailing resort of **Dartmouth** *(p105)*, also filled with reminders of the Elizabethan era. From Totnes or Dartmouth, it is an easy excursion to the **South Hams**. Unless you are based in Totnes or Dartmouth, either stay over in **Kingsbridge** or **Salcombe** *(p105)*, or head back up the A381 to **Exeter** *(p38)*.

The Best of the Rest

Hiker admiring the view from Berry Head

1. Berry Head, Torbay

K5

This sweeping coastal headland and nature reserve is home to guillemots and the endangered greater horseshoe bat.

2. Fairlynch Museum

L4 27 Fore St, Budleigh Salterton Apr–Oct: 2–4:30pm Tue–Sun & bank hols fairlynchmuseum.uk

Housed in a 19th-century *cottage orné* (decorated cottage), this museum has an impressive collection of lace, period costumes and vintage toys.

3. Beer Quarry Caves

M4 Quarry Lane, Beer Apr–Oct: 10am–4:30pm daily beerquarrycaves.co.uk

This limestone quarry, first established by the Romans, supplied stone for Exeter and St Paul's cathedrals. Note, it is open for guided tours only.

4. Bicton Park

L4 East Budleigh, Budleigh Salterton 10am–5pm daily bictongardens.co.uk

A horticultural idyll, Bicton includes a 1730s formal garden reputedly inspired by Versailles, and a Palm House from the 1820s.

5. Allhallows Museum

L3 High St, Honiton Apr–Oct: 9:30am–4:30pm Mon–Fri, 9:30am–1pm Sat; Nov & Dec: 10am–2pm Tue & Sat honitonmuseum.co.uk

Housed in the oldest building in Honiton, this museum displays fine lace.

6. Overbeck's Garden

J6 Sharpitor, Salcombe Mid-Feb–Oct: 10:30am–4pm Sun–Thu nationaltrust.org.uk

A subtropical oasis in the grounds of inventor Otto Overbeck's former home.

7. Otterton Mill

L4 Otterton, Budleigh Salterton 9:30am–4pm daily ottertonmill.com

Explore this working mill's historic buildings, then visit its gallery, farm shop and restaurant before enjoying a scenic stroll along the River Otter.

8. Kingsbridge Cookworthy Museum

J6 108 Fore St, Kingsbridge Apr–Oct: 10:30am–3:30pm Mon–Fri kingsbridgemuseum.org.uk

Named after the pioneer of English porcelain made from china clay, this local history museum offers a glimpse into the region's mining heritage.

9. Burgh Island

J6 Bigbury-on-Sea

Accessible by sea tractor at high tide, this tiny isle is home to the ritzy Burgh Island Hotel *(p119)*.

10. Plymouth Gin Distillery

P5 60 Southside St 11am–4:30pm Mon, 11am–5:30pm Tue–Sat, noon–5pm Sun plymouthdistillery.com

Housed in the Black Friar's building, this is England's oldest working gin distillery. Tours include tastings.

Towns and Villages

1. Salcombe
J6

At the mouth of the Kingsbridge Estuary, Devon's southernmost port is a magnet for sailors and tourists alike, becoming very busy during peak season.

2. Totnes
K5

The age of this riverside town is attested by its Norman castle and medieval remains. It has an alternative vibe and has long been popular with craftworkers.

3. Brixham
K5

Much of the seafood served in the region's restaurants is landed at this harbour. A replica of the Golden Hind, the vessel in which Francis Drake circumnavigated the globe, is moored here.

4. Budleigh Salterton
L4

John Everett Millais painted his famous *Boyhood of Raleigh* while on this village's pebble beach.

5. Sidmouth
L4

This pretty resort town has a long esplanade fronted by a shingle strand. Families prefer the more secluded Jacob's Ladder beach to the west.

6. Dartmouth
K6

The Royal Regatta *(p106)* and the Royal Naval College confirm this port's yachting credentials. Cobbled streets, impressive Tudor buildings and a castle add to its allure.

7. Beer
M4

This village is best-known for fishing, smuggling and Beer stone, a prized building material. A culvert carries a stream along the main street, from where you descend to the beach.

8. Cockington
K5

There is no denying the rustic appeal of this well-preserved village, a peaceful contrast to the ebullience of neighbouring Torquay.

9. Exmouth
L4

Primarily a family resort, Exmouth becomes quite lively during the summer. The Beacon, an elegant row of Regency houses overlooking the sea, once accommodated the wives of Byron and Nelson.

10. Torquay
K5

Capital of the so-called English Riviera, engaging Torquay, with its palms and fairy lights, feels almost Mediterranean.

Relaxing on the beach at Sidmouth

Sights Along the River Dart

Gothic façade of Buckfast Abbey

1. Buckfast Abbey

J5 Buckfastleigh 7:45am–8:20pm daily (to 7pm Sat) buckfast.org.uk

The River Exe flows through the grounds of this Benedictine house. The monks here produce tonic wine.

2. Dartington Hall

J5 Upper Drive, Totnes dartington.org

Founded by US heiress Dorothy Elmhirst, this arts and education centre hosts various cultural events.

3. Totnes Museum

K5 70 Fore St, Totnes Apr–Sep: 10:30am–4pm Tue & Fri totnesmuseum.org

Housed in a 1575 cloth merchant's home, this museum has a room devoted to Charles Babbage, who built the forerunner of the modern computer.

4. South Devon Railway

J5 Dart Bridge Rd, Buckfastleigh Apr–Oct: daily southdevonrailway.co.uk

Travel back in time in a vintage Great Western Railway coach hauled by a steam locomotive via the scenic route between Totnes and Buckfastleigh.

5. Totnes Guildhall

K5 5 Rampart's Walk 01803 862147 Apr–Oct: 11am–3pm Mon–Fri

Built on the ruins of a priory in 1553, the Guildhall later housed a courtroom and jail. It displays a table believed to have been used by Oliver Cromwell.

6. Riverlink Cruises

K5 5 Lower St, Dartmouth Apr–Oct: daily dartmouthrailriver.co.uk

The most relaxing way to explore the Dart is during a 90-minute cruise between Totnes and Dartmouth.

7. Greenway

J6 Galmpton Mar–Dec: hours vary; book parking in advance nationaltrust.org.uk

Set on the riverbank, Agatha Christie's holiday home, furnished in 1950s style, is full of her family's collections of books, china and more.

8. South Devon Chilli Farm

J6 Loddiswell, near Kingsbridge Hours vary, check website southdevonchillifarm.co.uk

Home to over 200 varieties of chilli, this farm showcases many of them growing in season. There's also a café and a shop.

9. Dartmouth Royal Regatta

K5 dartmouthregatta.co.uk

Held in late August, this annual four-day jamboree celebrates the port's rich history and maritime traditions with colourful pageantry.

10. Dartmouth Museum

K5 The Butterwalk, Duke St, Dartmouth 11am–3pm daily dartmouthmuseum.org

Themed rooms in this museum explore the town's maritime history with model ships, paintings and other memorabilia.

Places to Eat

1. The Elephant

K5 3 & 4 Beacon Terrace, Torquay Sun–Tue elephantrestaurant.co.uk • ££

This Michelin-starred spot offers dishes made with local ingredients, including vegetables grown on the chef's farm.

2. Lympstone Manor

L4 Courtlands Lane, Exmouth lympstonemanor.co.uk • £££

A venture by culinary genius Michael Caines, this boutique country hotel has three restaurants and a vineyard.

3. Riverford Field Kitchen

J5 Wash Farm, Buckfastleigh 01803 227391 Mon, Tue & D Sat • ££

A friendly, organic farm restaurant, serving hearty lunches and dinners at wooden communal tables.

4. Rockfish

K6 8 South Embankment, Dartmouth 01803 832800 • ££

The first branch of chef and writer Mitch Tonks' seafood restaurant is laid-back yet chic. Try the fish tacos or go for the traditional fish and chips that comes with unlimited chips.

5. Café Alf Resco

K5 Lower St, Dartmouth D Daily cafealfresco.co.uk • £

A local favourite, this child-friendly café with a terrace serves pastries, baguettes and lunchtime specials.

Spacious dining room at Rockfish

PRICE CATEGORIES

For a three-course meal for one with half a bottle of wine, including taxes and extra charges.

£ under £35 ££ £35–£55 £££ over £55

6. The Curator

K5 2 The Plains, Totnes D Daily thecurator.co.uk • £

Along with superb wood-roasted speciality coffee, this café also serves Italian-inspired breakfasts, lunches, pastries and cakes.

7. Gidleigh Park

J4 Chagford gidleigh.co.uk • £££

Ian Webber is the latest chef to lead this Michelin-starred kitchen. His menu combines Far East influences with an excellent selection of meticulously sourced local ingredients.

8. The Pig at Combe

L3 Gittisham, Honiton thepighotel.com/at-combe • ££

Set in a romantic Elizabethan manor, this hotel has a restaurant that sources its vegetables from its own kitchen garden. It also offers outdoor seating.

9. Barbican Kitchen

Q6 60 Southside St, Plymouth 01752 604448 Sun & Mon • ££

Set in the historic Plymouth Gin Distillery *(p104)*, this relaxed brasserie is famed for its Friday fish and chips, using the day's catch fresh from the boats at Looe in Cornwall.

10. The Seahorse

K6 5 South Embankment, Dartmouth Sun & Mon seahorserestaurant.co.uk • £££

Mitch Tonks' flagship restaurant specializes in fresh fish and shellfish grilled on an open charcoal fire. There are excellent-value lunch and early dinner menus.

STREETSMART

Dartmouth Steam Railway, Devon

4277

GETTING AROUND

Whether you're visiting Cornwall and Devon for a short break or week-long country retreat, discover how best to reach your destination and travel around like a pro.

AT A GLANCE

TRAIN TRAVEL COSTS

DAY RANGER TICKETS

£17

One day's unlimited rail travel

FREEDOM OF DEVON AND CORNWALL

£67

Unlimited rail travel for 3 days out of 7

FREEDOM OF DEVON AND CORNWALL

£107.50

Unlimited rail travel for 8 days out of 15

SPEED LIMITS

MOTORWAY

70 mph (110 km/h)

DUAL CARRIAGEWAYS

70 mph (110 km/h)

SINGLE CARRIAGEWAYS

60 mph (95 km/h)

URBAN AREAS

30 mph (45 km/h)

Arriving by Air

International flights arrive into London and regular flights from Europe also serve Southampton and Bristol airports. South West England's main airport is **Exeter Airport**, with direct flights from several UK and European cities. **Cornwall Airport Newquay** and **Land's End Airport** have flights to St Mary's Airport in the Scilly Isles, and there are seasonal flights from Exeter; **Skybus** runs all flights to the Scilly Isles.

A bus service from Land's End Airport to Penzance railway station is operated for Skybus passengers. Mini-buses meet arrivals at St Mary's Airport, with transfers around the island.

Cornwall Airport Newquay
W cornwallairportnewquay.com
Exeter Airport
W exeter-airport.co.uk
Land's End Airport
W landsendairport.co.uk
Skybus
W islesofscilly-travel.co.uk/skybus

International Train Travel

St Pancras International is the London terminus for **Eurostar**, the high-speed train linking the UK with Paris, Brussels and Amsterdam. **Eurotunnel** operates a drive-on-drive-off train service between Calais and Folkestone.

Eurostar
W eurostar.com
Eurotunnel
W leshuttle.com

Domestic Train Travel

Great Western Railway runs trains (both daytime and sleeper services) from London Paddington to Penzance, taking approximately 5 hours and usually calling at Exeter, Totnes, Plymouth, Liskeard, Truro and St Erth. There is also a **Southwestern Railway** link between London Waterloo and Exeter (approximately three hours).

Branch lines also connect numerous towns around Cornwall and Devon by train. Useful lines include the routes from Exeter south to Torquay and Paignton and north to Barnstaple; from Liskeard, a line heads to Looe; from Par, trains run north to Newquay; and from Truro, a line goes to Falmouth. Note that tickets are usually cheaper when bought in advance.

Great Western Railway
W gwr.com
Southwestern Railway
W southerwesternrailway.com

Long-Distance Bus Travel

National Express coaches run from London to Penzance, but the trip takes around nine hours. There are also services to destinations such as Exeter, Truro and Falmouth. Book in advance.

National Express
W nationalexpress.com

Buses

Buses are a cheap way to get around Cornwall and Devon, though services can be irregular. Buses operated by **Stagecoach** connect Exeter Airport with Exeter St David's railway station, Exeter bus station and Exmouth. There is also a regular bus service between Cornwall Airport Newquay, Newquay railway station and Padstow, run by **First Kernow**.

There are numerous companies in Devon (listed on **Travel Devon**), while in Cornwall most services are run by First Kernow, with a few local operators (listed on **Transport for Cornwall**).

First Kernow
W firstbus.co.uk/cornwall
Stagecoach
W stagecoachbus.com
Travel Devon
W traveldevon.info
Transport for Cornwall
W transportforcornwall.co.uk

Driving

Driving around Cornwall and Devon is the most convenient way to explore this region, particularly if you're venturing to rural areas. However, drivers should allow plenty of time to reach their destinations: roads can be windy and narrow, and satnavs are not always reliable. Traffic can also be an issue, particularly during the summer and on bank holiday weekends.

Ferries

From mid-March to October, **Isles of Scilly Travel** runs ferries from Penzance to the islands while **Lundy Shore Office** operates a seasonal service to Lundy Island from Ilfracombe and Bideford.

Local car ferries across rivers and estuaries often save drivers a detour. The Kingswear Ferry connects to Dartmouth, while the King Harry chain ferry between the Roseland Peninsula and Trelissick saves drivers 43 km (27 miles). C Toms and Son runs a car ferry between Fowey and Bodinnick. Padstow Ferry shuttles passengers between Padstow and Rock, and in the summer months Mevagissey Ferries runs a passenger ferry between Fowey and Mevagissey.

Isles of Scilly Travel
W islesofscilly-travel.co.uk
Lundy Shore Office
W landmarktrust.org.uk

Cycling

There are plenty of cycling routes in the area. Off-road routes include the Granite Way on Dartmoor, the Tarka Trail, the flat Camel Trail and the Saints Way *(p58)*. Excellent cycle maps and guides of the National Cycle Network are published by **Sustrans**.

Sustrans
W sustrans.org.uk

Walking

Cornwall and Devon are prime walking territory. The epic **South West Coast Path** snakes along the entire South West Peninsula, while numerous scenic inland hikes await in Bodmin Moor, Exmoor and Dartmoor. Before heading out, always make sure you are well equipped and prepared for all weather.

South West Coast Path
W southwestcoastpath.org.uk

PRACTICAL INFORMATION

A little local know-how goes a long way in Cornwall and Devon. On these pages you can find all the essential advice and information you will need to make the most of your trip to this region.

CURRENCY
Pound Sterling (GBP)

AVERAGE DAILY SPEND

SAVE
£70

SPEND
£140

SPLURGE
£230

CLIMATE

The longest days occur May–Aug, while Nov–Feb sees the lowest daylight hours.

Temperatures average 22 °C (75 °F) in summer. Winter can be cold and icy.

October and November see the most rainfall, but heavy showers occur all year round.

ELECTRICITY SUPPLY

Power sockets are type G, fitting three-pronged plugs. Standard voltage is 230 volts.

Passports and Visas

For entry requirements, including visas, consult your nearest British embassy or check the **UK Government** website. Post-Brexit arrangements for citizens from EEA countries will vary depending on the terms agreed; rights of Irish citizens will not change. Citizens of the US, Canada, Australia and New Zealand do not need visas for stays of up to six months. Any visitors who do not hold British or Irish citizenship may need to apply for an electronic travel authorisation (**ETA**) before arriving.

ETA
W gov.uk/guidance/apply-for-an-electronic-travel-authorisation-eta

UK Government
W gov.uk

Government Advice

Now more than ever, it is important to consult both your and the UK government's advice before travelling. The UK Foreign, Commonwealth & Development Office (**FCDO**), the **US Department of State** and the **Australian Department of Foreign Affairs and Trade** offer the latest information on security, health and local regulations.

Australian Department of Foreign Affairs and Trade
W smartraveller.gov.au

FCDO
W gov.uk /foreign-travel-advice

US Department of State
W travel.state.gov

Customs Information

You can find information on the laws relating to goods and currency taken in or out of the UK on the **UK Government** website.

UK Government
W gov.uk/duty-free-goods

Insurance

We recommend that you take out a comprehensive insurance policy covering theft, loss of belongings, medical care, cancellations and delays, and read the small print carefully.

Emergency treatment is usually free from the National Health Service (**NHS**) for UK residents, and there are reciprocal arrangements with Australia, New Zealand and some other countries (check the NHS website for the latest details). Healthcare arrangements for EEA citizens are subject to change; check the NHS website for the most up-to-date information.

NHS
W nhs-services

Vaccinations

No inoculations are required to visit the UK.

Money

The currency in the UK is the pound sterling (GBP). Major credit and debit cards, plus contactless payments, are widely accepted. Some smaller businesses, markets and local public transport, however, operate a cash-only policy.

In restaurants it's customary to tip 10–15 per cent for good service. It is usual to tip taxi drivers 10 per cent, and concierges, hotel porters and housekeeping £1–2 per bag or day.

Travellers with Specific Requirements

Tourism for All is the UK's central source of travel information for those with specific requirements. Most modern buildings and infrastructure in Cornwall and Devon have been designed with wheelchairs in mind, but many old buildings in the region have not yet been adapted, so be sure to check relevant websites in advance.

Most trains in the UK have been adapted to take wheelchairs and offer assistance services, and many local buses have low floors to accommodate wheelchairs; however it is worth checking specific services ahead of travel.

Many major museums and galleries offer audio tours and induction loops for those with impaired sight and hearing. The **Royal National Institute for Deaf People** (RNID) and the **Royal National Institute of Blind People** offer information and advice.

Countryside Mobility South West rents mobility equipment – such as all-terrain scooters – at several sites. **Accessible Countryside** also features a list of walks suitable for wheelchair users across the region.

Accessible Countryside
W accessiblecountryside.org.uk
Countryside Mobility South West
W countrysidemobility.org
Royal National Institute for Deaf People
W rnid.org.uk
Royal National Institute of Blind People
W rnib.org.uk
Tourism for All
W tourismforall.co.uk

Language

English is spoken throughout Cornwall and Devon. Accents vary tremendously, and can be stronger in certain areas.

Opening Hours

Major supermarkets are generally open from 8am to 8pm. Other shops usually open between 9am and 10am and close at 5 or 5:30pm. On Sundays, most shops are restricted to opening for only six hours, generally from 10am to 4pm.

Banks usually open 9am or 9:30am to 3:30 or 4pm weekdays. Some branches also open on Saturday mornings.

Museums usually open between 9 and 10am and close between 4 and 6pm. Some close on Mondays.

On bank holidays, banks close and some shops and attractions either close or operate shorter hours.

Situations can change quickly and unexpectedly. Always check before visiting attractions and hospitality venues for up-to-date opening hours and booking requirements.

Personal Security

Cornwall and Devon are both safe areas to visit, with theft and crime relatively rare. Use your common sense and take the usual precautions.

If you have anything stolen, report the crime as soon as possible to the nearest police station. Get a copy of the crime report in order to claim on your insurance. Contact your embassy if your passport is stolen or in the event of a serious crime or accident.

On the whole, England is welcoming and inclusive, with many nationalities calling the country home and some of the most progressive LGBTQ+ rights in Europe. Homosexuality was legalized in England in 1967 and the UK recognized the right to legally change your gender in 2004. Even so, acceptance is not necessarily a given and communities can feel quite homogenous outside of major cities. If you do feel unsafe, the **Safe Space Alliance** pinpoints your nearest place of refuge.

Be careful around the sea as currents can change quickly. Never enter the water when a red warning flag is flying. To locate beaches supervised by a lifeguard, visit the **Royal National Lifeboat Institution** (RNLI) website.

Royal National Lifeboat Institution
W rnli.org

Safe Space Alliance
W safespacealliance.com

Health

The UK has a world-class healthcare system and emergency medical care is generally free. Visitors from abroad may have to pay upfront for medical treatment and reclaim on insurance at a later date. It is therefore important to arrange comprehensive medical insurance before you travel.

For minor ailments go to a pharmacy or chemist. These are plentiful in towns and cities. You may need a doctor's prescription to obtain certain pharmaceuticals; the pharmacist can inform you of the closest doctor's surgery or medical centre where you can see a GP (general practitioner).

If you have an accident or a medical problem requiring non-urgent medical attention, find details of your nearest non-emergency medical service on the NHS website. Alternatively, contact **NHS 111** (the NHS emergency care service) at any hour online or by phone.

AT A GLANCE

EMERGENCY NUMBERS

GENERAL EMERGENCY	POLICE (NON-EMERGENCY)	MEDICAL (NON-EMERGENCY)
999	101	111

TIME ZONE

GMT/BST
British Summer Time (BST) runs late March to late October.

TAP WATER

Unless otherwise stated, tap water in the UK is safe to drink.

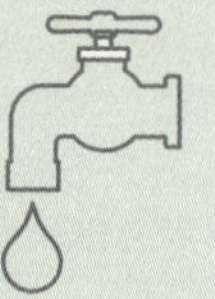

WEBSITES AND APPS

Visit Cornwall
The region's official tourist board website (*www.visitcornwall.com*).

Visit Devon
The region's official tourist board website (*www.visitdevon.co.uk*).

Visit Isles of Scilly
The region's official tourist board website (*www.visitislesofscilly.com*).

what3words
Pinpoint your exact location with this app.

If things are serious, call 999 or go to your nearest Accident and Emergency (A&E) department.

Hikers might pick up ticks, which can carry Lyme disease; if you see a tick on your body, contact a doctor or pharmacist promptly.

NHS 111
W 111.nhs.uk

Smoking, Alcohol and Drugs

Smoking and vaping are banned in all enclosed public spaces. However, many bars and restaurants have outdoor areas where smoking is permitted.

Alcohol may not be sold to or bought for anyone under 18. The UK legal limit for drivers is 80 mg of alcohol per 100 ml of blood, or 0.08 per cent BAC (blood alcohol content). This is roughly equivalent to one small glass of wine or a pint of regular-strength lager. It is best to avoid drinking altogether if you plan to drive.

Possession of any recreational drugs could result in a prison sentence.

ID

There is no requirement for visitors to carry ID, but in the case of a routine check you may be asked to show your passport and visa documentation. Anyone who looks under 18 (or in some cases, under 25) may be asked for photo ID when buying alcohol.

Responsible Tourism

England's **Countryside Code** sets out the responsibilities of visitors to the countryside, including keeping dogs under control and leaving gates and property as you found them. Ensure that you leave no trace when visiting nature spots and take away your litter.

Take care to mitigate the impact of overtourism in the area by engaging with local businesses and tour guides, cycling and using public transport where possible, and visiting out of season.

Countryside Code
W gov.uk/government/publications/the-countryside-code

Mobile Phones and Wi-Fi

Free Wi-Fi hotspots are widely available in town and city centres. Many train stations also offer free Wi-Fi.

Visitors from outside the UK should check whether they are affected by data roaming charges; it may be cheaper to buy a SIM card in the UK.

Do not rely on mobile phones or other devices for navigation or emergency communications in remote areas, where reception can be intermittent or non-existent.

Postal Services

Standard post in the UK is handled by **Royal Mail**. Post office branches are found in most towns and cities. Stamps are available in post offices, supermarkets and newsagents. The Royal Mail website provides full details on charges.

Royal Mail
W royalmail.com

Taxes and Refunds

VAT (Value Added Tax) is charged at 20 per cent and almost always included in the marked price. Visitors to Britain are only able to buy goods tax-free in shops if they are shipped to an address outside the UK; check with the retailer if they offer this service.

Discount Cards

Most attractions offer concessionary rates for children, seniors and students. If you are a student, the International Student Identity Card (**ISIC**) is recommended. If you intend to visit several castles, homes and gardens, a **National Trust** membership may be worthwhile. Also worth considering is a **Cornwall Heritage Trust** membership, which gives free entry to English Heritage attractions in Cornwall, plus discounted entry to several other historic sites.

Cornwall Heritage Trust
W cornwallheritagetrust.org

ISIC
W isic.org

National Trust
W nationaltrust.org.uk

PLACES TO STAY

Cornwall and Devon are full of memorable places to stay, from clifftop campsites with soaring views to high-end hotels housed in historic fortresses.

Second homes and buy-to-let properties have driven up prices for locals in both counties; to avoid contributing to the problem, opt for campsites, hostels, B&Bs, guesthouses and hotels instead. With everything from self-catering coastal aparthotels to country estates with Michelin-starred dining on offer, you won't be sacrificing a thing.

PRICE CATEGORIES

For a standard, double room per night (with breakfast if included), taxes and extra charges.

£ under £100
££ £100–£200
£££ over £200

North Cornwall

SeaSpace

C4 Watergate Rd, Porth sea.space · ££

With views straight over the Atlantic from numerous rooms, the aparthotel SeaSpace lives up to its name. It's housed in a restored Art Deco building, with bright and airy decor complementing the large sea-facing windows. And while it's located just outside Newquay's centre, nearly everything you'll need is here: there's a café, restaurant, pool, gym and a small shop for self-catering supplies.

Michael House

D3 Trelake Ln, Treknow michael-house.co.uk · £

Guests can expect a warm welcome at this intimate B&B (there are just two rooms) run by Vanessa and Simon. Its location couldn't be better – near Tintagel and a host of coastal walks – but that's not even the best part. Vanessa's delicious vegan cooking (using some ingredients fresh from the garden) is worth the trip alone.

YHA Boscastle

D2 Palace Stables, Boscastle yha.org.uk · £

Walking the South West Coast Path? Pitstop at this lovely little YHA, located on Boscastle's quayside, right on the trail. The hostel features dorms with shared bathrooms and private rooms with en-suite facilities.

The St Enodoc Hotel

D3 Rock enodoc hotel.co.uk · £££

Fans of coastal-chic interior design look no further. Located in the village of Rock, this boutique hotel is handsomely decked out in blue and green hues, with many rooms offering extensive estuary views. Amenities are top-notch, too: guests can unwind in the spa, feast on local food washed down with Cornish wine in the on-site brasserie or relax on the beach (on the hotel's doorstop). The charming town of Padstow is just a short boat ride away.

St Benet's Abbey

D4 Truro Rd, Lanivet, Bodmin stbenets abbey.co.uk · ££

Constructed in 1411, this medieval house-turned-B&B makes for an atmospheric place to stay in the heart of the Cornish countryside. It's historical features include four-poster beds and stained-glass windows while its leafy garden is the perfect spot for relaxing in the sun.

The Scarlet

C4 Tredragon Rd, Mawgan Porth scarlet hotel.co.uk · £££

Nestled in the cliffs above Mawgan Porth beach, this stylish eco hotel promises everything you need to switch off: log-fired hot tubs, a natural swimming pool and an Ayurvedic spa. There's also a gorgeous restaurant which serves up local produce. It's strictly grown-ups only, and makes for the ultimate romantic retreat.

Watergate Bay Hotel

C4 Watergate Bay watergatebay.co.uk · £££

Located on Watergate Bay – an area famed for its big waves and top surf school, Wavehunters – this beachfront hotel is always a hit with surfers. But don't feel obliged to take to the waves: the ocean-facing pool and lovely sauna promise a much more relaxing afternoon. Self-catering is also available.

South Cornwall

The Idle Rocks

C5 Harbourside, St Mawes idlerocks.com · £££

Fancy an indulgent weekend in St Mawes? Look no further than this chic conversion of an Edwardian waterfront inn. The interior is fabulous, adorned with colourful paintings, driftwood sculptures and collections of vintage bathing suits. Meanwhile, the restaurant uses only the freshest local ingredients and the south-facing terrace is perfect for admiring the view.

Coverack Camping

C6 Penmarth Farm, Coverack coverackcamping.co.uk · £

Set in a stunning clifftop location overlooking Coverack Cove, this pretty campsite is run by the Roskilly family (of Roskilly's ice cream fame). It's a no-frills, eco-friendly site, with compost toilets and solar-powered showers. However, you can opt for a little more luxury by booking a cosy pre-erected Celtic Pod or Longhouse Tent.

The Rosevine

C5 Rosevine, North Portscatho rosevine.co.uk · ££

This country house combines the comforts of a luxury hotel with the independence of self-catering. It's set in luxuriant gardens, just above a sheltered sandy cove, and features a playroom, an indoor heated pool, an adults-only lounge and a good restaurant. For those who'd rather cook their own meals, the studios, apartments and suites all have a kitchen and dining area.

Talland Bay Hotel

E4 Porthallow tallandbayhotel.co.uk · £££

Art abounds in this small luxury hotel, with each room and self-catering cottage decorated with quirky pieces, courtesy of the artist-in-residence. This attention to detail isn't just confined to the rooms, however. Meals at the restaurant are inventive, cocktails are unique and specially crafted, and the idyllic view of the sea, framed by the garden, is a work of art in its own right.

House on the Props

E4 Talland St, Polperro houseonprops.co.uk · £

You can't get closer to the harbour than this B&B: as the name suggests, the building is partially on struts over the water, and two of the three rooms look right out over jostling masts. Unsurprisingly, seafood is the order of the day in the restaurant, but there are vegan options, too.

West Cornwall and the Isles of Scilly

Henry's Campsite

C6 The Lizard henryscampsite.co.uk · £

This colourful campsite has personality in spades. Wildflowers and exotic plants create a lush backdrop while hand-painted wood art is dotted around the grounds and free-roaming ducks make frequent appearances. All pitches have electric hook-ups, and some have sea views.

Artist Residence Cornwall

B5 Chapel St, Penzance artistresidence.co.uk/cornwall · ££

Housed in a restored Georgian building, this award-winning hotel is decorated in a cool, lived-in nautical style that never veers into cliché. The cosy bar and restaurant and gorgeous terrace garden are highlights, too.

YHA Penzance

B5 Castle Horneck, Penzance yha.org.uk · £

Located in an old Georgian mansion, the YHA Penzance has everything you could ask for from a hostel: a range of rooms (from dorms to doubles to campsites), a self-catering kitchen, affordable breakfast and super-friendly staff. It's also got the added bonus of chandeliers, a stunning staircase and a porticoed entrance.

Hell Bay

A4 Bryher, Isles of Scilly hellbay.co.uk · £££

Want to get away from it all? Escape to this modern hotel, set above a rugged bay on remote Bryher island. Leaving the crowds doesn't mean skimping on luxury, though. There's an outdoor heated swimming pool, a spa, a yoga studio and locally sourced food in the restaurant. It's an excellent spot for families, too, with outdoor activities like pitch and put, a giant chess set and board games for rainy days.

Hotel Meudon

C5 Maenporth Rd, Mawnan Smith meudon.co.uk · ££

There are numerous things to write home about the Hotel Meudon: its bright, comfortable rooms, inventive dinner and drinks menus and elegant afternoon teas, to name just a few. But the real star here is the location. The hotel is set in its own valley where subtropical plants grow in startling profusion and the garden tumbles down towards a secluded, pebbly cove. It's a veritable oasis.

Old Success Inn

A5 Cove Hill, Sennen Cove oldsuccess.co.uk · ££

With good vibes, good beer and good grub, the Old Success Inn is a hard pub to leave. Luckily, you don't have to. This beloved boozer also hosts a number of cosy rooms, decorated in calming Cornish colours (think shades of sand, pebble and sea) that provide the perfect antidote to a few too many pints at the pub.

Star Castle Hotel

B4 St Mary's, Isles of Scilly starcastle.co.uk · £££

Live like a royal in this star-shaped fortress, built on the orders of Elizabeth I. Inside, it's all wood-beamed ceilings, creaky staircases and crooked rooms furnished with Persian rugs and Jacobean-style furniture. Yet there are more contemporary touches, too. Along with a pool and tennis courts, Star Castle houses two restaurants and a bar, which make use of the abundant local produce and wine from the hotel's own HolyVale Vineyard *(p42)*.

North Devon

Epchris House

H1 Torrs Park, Ilfracombe epchrisguesthouse.co.uk · £

This relaxed, dog-friendly B&B is elevated by thoughtful touches like room-service breakfasts (with vegan and gluten-free options), e-bike charging facilities and even a complimentary afternoon tea. Staff can also arrange seal-spotting scuba trips to nearby Lundy Island.

Livit Adventures and Glamping

H2 Westacott Farm, Abbotsham livitadventures.com · £

Make the most of the great outdoors at this glampsite near Bideford. The owners are full of recommendations for local walking, swimming and climbing spots; they also run surfing lessons and cook up wood-fired pizzas on the weekend.

The Beach at Bude

E2 Summerleaze Crescent, Bude thebeachatbude.co.uk · ££

Guests only ever have great things to say about this seaside hotel, particularly when it comes to the staff. The folks at The Beach go above and beyond to make every stay special, whether you're celebrating a birthday (they'll probably leave you a card) or simply enjoying a meal at the restaurant (service is always top-notch).

The Collective at Woolsery

G2 Chapel St, Woolfardisworthy woolsery.com · £££

The Collective is less a hotel, more an impeccably designed village. There are the rooms, suites and cottages, all decorated in a luxurious mid-century style, but there's also a gourmet pub (the Farmers Arms), a laid-back chippy, a village store and a post office. A vast farm, with an emphasis on rewilding, supplies the site.

Saunton Sands Hotel

H1 Saunton Rd, Braunton saunton sands.co.uk · £££

Housed in an elegant Art Deco building, Saunton Sands Hotel promises old-school luxury, right by the beach. There's an on-site spa with a wide range of facilities and treatments, one indoor and one outdoor pool, a gym and a children's playroom (with childcare available). Dining options run the gamut from classic afternoon teas to River Exe mussels served on the terrace.

South Devon

Four Seasons Guest House

K5 Bridgetown, Totnes fourseasons totnes.co.uk · £

This cosy B&B in Totnes taps into the town's creative, eco-friendly atmosphere. You'll see works by local artists on the walls and your breakfast will include seasonal home-grown fruit, straight from the kitchen garden.

YHA Okehampton

H3 Klondyke Rd, Okehampton yha.org.uk · £

Ideally located next door to Okehampton station, this no-frills hostel is a great spot for walkers. Numerous trails are within easy access, many leading you deep into the wilds of Dartmoor.

Soar Mill Cove Hotel

J6 Soar Mill Cove, Salcombe soarmillcove.co.uk · ££

Looking to book a family holiday? Bag one of the self-catering villas at Soar Mill Cove. A short drive from buzzy Salcombe and within easy reach of numerous family-friendly beaches, this welcoming hotel makes for an ideal base to explore the local area. The hotel itself has plenty to offer, too – kids will love the tennis court and games room.

Burgh Island Hotel

J6 Burgh Island, Bigbury-on-Sea burgh island.com · £££

With a 1930s billiards room, gorgeous cocktail bar and swoonworthy swimming lagoon, this dreamy island getaway oozes Art Deco elegance. Numerous famous guests have stayed here, too, including Agatha Christie and Winston Churchill; in honour of the former, murder mystery parties are a frequent – and always fun – occurrence.

Gidleigh Park

J4 Chagford gidleigh.co.uk · £££

Perfect for honeymoons, this romantic haven is located in a striking half-timbered Tudor-style house, set amid acres of private woodland in Dartmoor National Park.

Lympstone Manor

L4 Courtlands Ln, Exmouth lympstone manor.co.uk · £££

This two-Michelin Key hotel makes the most of its stunning Georgian building, extensive gardens and gorgeous location overlooking the River Exe. You can stay in one of the main house's tastefully decorated rooms, or opt for a cosy, colourful shepherd hut in the woodland. Set aside plenty of time for food and drink – the restaurant has its own Michelin credentials, and there's even a vineyard in the grounds.

Southernhay House

K3 36 Southernhay East, Exeter southern hayhouse.com · £££

This luxurious townhouse in Exeter's Georgian quarter features monsoon showers and mid-room rolltop baths, giving the rooms a boudoir-feel. There's also a cocktail bar and great restaurant.

INDEX

Page numbers in **bold** refer to main entries.

N

O

P

U

V

W

Y

ACKNOWLEDGMENTS

This edition updated by

Contributor Rebecca Hallett

Senior Editors Keith Drew, Alison McGill

Senior Designers Katie Cavanagh, Laura O'Brien, Stuti Tiwari, Vinita Venugopal

Project Editor Lucy Sara-Kelly

Art Editor Sulagna Das

Editors Molly McCarthy, Anuroop Sanwalia, Vineet Singh

Proofreader Ben Ffrancon Dowds

Indexer Helen Peters

Deputy Picture Research Manager Virien Chopra

Senior Picture Researcher Nishwan Rasool

Assistant Picture Research Administrator Manpreet Kaur

Publishing Assistant Simona Velikova

Jacket Designers Cristina Antequera, Laura O'Brien

Jacket Picture Researcher Naomi McMullen

Senior Cartographer Subhashree Bharati

Senior Cartographic Editor James Macdonald

Cartography Manager Suresh Kumar

Pre-Production Coordinator Tanveer Zaidi

Pre-Production Image Editors Jagtar Singh, Vijay Khandwal, Ashok Kumar

Pre-Production Manager Balwant Singh

Pre-Production Image Manager Pankaj Sharma

Production Controller Kariss Ainsworth

Deputy Managing Editor Dharini Ganesh

Managing Editor Beverly Smart

Managing Art Editor Gemma Doyle

Senior Managing Art Editor Priyanka Thakur

Editorial Director Hollie Teague

Art Director Maxine Pedliham

Publishing Director Georgina Dee

DK would like to thank the following for their contribution to the previous editions: Robert Andrews, Ros Belford, Elizabeth Dale, Norm Longley, Laura Walker.

The publisher would like to thank the following for their kind permission to reproduce their photographs:

Key: a-above; b-below/bottom; c-center; f-far; l-left; r-right; t-top

4Corners: Dave Porter 104.

Adobe Stock: hardyuno 75b, 82–83b.

Alamy Stock Photo: Aitan 39cb; ArchivalSurvival 79; Kevin Britland 20cla, 71; Adam Burton 15clb, 17, 81; David Chapman 88t, 95; Chronicle 50t; Classic Image 8; Craig Joiner Photography 98; Richard Cummins 85; David Gee 4 39br, 101b; Helen Dixon 16cla; Greg Balfour Evans 15crb; eye35.pix 58–59b; Thomas Faull 63; David Forster 20cra; Tony French 9tr; Horst Friedrichs 13cla, 34b, 65; funkyfood London - Paul Williams 46–47b; Joseph Gaul 67; June Green 20br; Rik Hamilton 49; Marc Hill 10cl; James Hodgson 14; Iconographic Archive 41; image 22b, 23b; Image Professionals GmbH / LOOK-foto 22–23t; imageBROKER / Angela to Roxel 54; imageBROKER.com / Paul Williams - FunkyStock 12br, 91; Christopher Jones 52t; Douglas Lander 32cla, 39crb, 105; De Luan 9tl; mauritius images GmbH / Martin Siepmann 82t; mauritius images GmbH / Steve Vidler 40, 62; Neil McAllister 103; Jim Monk 26–27; Christopher Nicholson 48, 52b, 55; Nathaniel Noir 93; North Wind Picture Archives 10tl; PA Images / Ben Birchall 94; Chris Pancewicz 75t; Lee Pengelly 1; Will Perrett 43t; Photimageon 13cl; Realimage 58t; Matthias Riedinger 92; robertharding / Adam Burton 36; G Scammell 70t; Gordon Scammell 13cl (8); Steve Taylor ARPS 64; Jack Sullivan 24cra; Nik Taylor 60b; The Picture Art Collection 9cr; travelbild 32–33b, 39bl, 109; travelib europe 29b; Steve Vidler 15t; Washington Imaging 97b; Matt Whorlow 21; World History Archive 10–11b, 12crb.

AWL Images: Robert Birkby 6–7, 42–43b, 56–57; Adam Burton 87; Alan Copson 13tl, 28, 78; Kav Dadfar 45; Jeremy Flint 102; Niels van Gijn 13bl; Gavin Hellier 96–97t; Nigel Pavitt 34–35t; Steve Vidler 106.

Dreamstime.com: Alexey Fedorenko 101t; Jessica Girvan 66, 99; Helen Hotson 59t, 68t; Aagje De Jong 24–25b; Judita Lіociene 47t; Tom Meaker 90; Travelling-light 77, 88–89b; Xantana 30–31.

Getty Images: AFP / - / Stringer 51; Hulton Archive / Fox Photos / Stringer 50b; Hulton

rchive / Print Collector 9br, Gav Goulder / In
ctures 11t; Moment Unreleased / Helmut Hess
4; The Image Bank Unreleased / Franz Marc Frei
2cr, 29t; The Image Bank Unreleased / Manfred
ottschalk 16tc.

etty Images / iStock: Peter Burnett 12cra;
ubfoto 5; Asdrubal Costa 16cr; E+ / JohnGollop
0bl; E+ / nicolamargaret 13clb; Thomas Faull 37;
uruJosh 76; Tom McAtee 60–61t; Lukas
Jrbaitis 15br.

ational Trust Images: Lynda Aiano 53.

Rockfish: 107.

Shutterstock.com: Mia Garrett 68–69b; Jory
Mundy 70b; Robert Harding Video 19, 38; Katie
Thorpe 73.

Cover images:

Front and Spine: **Getty Images:** Moment / Graham Custance Photography; *Back:* **Alamy Stock Photo:** funkyfood London - Paul Williams tr; imageBROKER.com / Paul Williams - FunkyStock tl; mauritius images GmbH / Steve Vidler cl.

Pull out map:

Getty Images: Moment / Graham Custance Photography.

A NOTE FROM DK

The rate at which the world is changing is constantly keeping the DK travel team on our toes. While we've worked hard to ensure that this edition of Cornwall and Devon is accurate and up-to-date, we know that opening hours alter, standards shift, prices fluctuate, places close and new ones pop up in their stead. So, if you notice we've got something wrong or left something out, we want to hear about it.Please get in touch at travelguides@dk.com

Within each Top 10 list in this book, no hierarchy of quality or popularity is implied. All 10 are, in the editor's opinion, of roughly equal merit.

First edition 2009

Published in Great Britain by Dorling Kindersley Limited, DK, 20 Vauxhall Bridge Road, London SW1V 2SA

The authorised representative in the EEA is Dorling Kindersley Verlag GmbH. Arnulfstr. 124, 80636 Munich, Germany

Published in the United States by DK Publishing, 1745 Broadway, 20th Floor, New York, NY 10019, USA

26 27 28 29 10 9 8 7 6 5 4 3 2 1

A CIP catalog record for this book is available from the British Library.

A catalog record for this book is available from the Library of Congress.

ISSN: 1479-344X
ISBN: 978 0 2417 8157 9

Printed and bound in China

www.dk.com

MIX
Paper | Supporting responsible forestry
FSC
www.fsc.org
FSC™ C018179

This book was made with Forest Stewardship Council™ certified paper – one small step in DK's commitment to a sustainable future.
Learn more at **www.dk.com/uk/information/sustainability**